The Rilke of Ruth Speirs

John Pilling has contributed essays and articles to *Poetry Nation Review* for more than thirty years, including several on Rainer Maria Rilke. His study *Fifty Modern European Poets* (Heinemann) was praised by figures as diverse as Joseph Brodsky and Peter Levi, but his principal focus as critic and editor has been on the prose fiction, poems and unpublished writings of Samuel Beckett. His poems have appeared in *Adam* and *Spectrum*, and he has translated from the work of Yves Bonnefoy, Eugenio Montale, and 'Der Nister'. He is Emeritus Professor of English and European Literature at the University of Reading.

Peter Robinson is the author of many books of poetry, translations, aphorisms, short fiction and literary criticism, and has been the recipient of the Cheltenham Prize, the John Florio Prize and two Poetry Book Society Recommendations. His most recent publications include *Foreigners, Drunks and Babies: Eleven Stories* (Two Rivers Press), a collection of poems, *Buried Music* (Shearsman Books) and *The Oxford Handbook of Contemporary British and Irish Poetry*, which he edited. He is Professor of English and American Literature at the University of Reading and poetry editor for Two Rivers Press.

The Rilke of Ruth Speirs

New Poems, Duino Elegies, Sonnets to Orpheus & Others

Edited by John Pilling & Peter Robinson

TWO
RIVERS
PRESS

First published in the UK in 2015 by Two Rivers Press
7 Denmark Road, Reading RG1 5PA.
www.tworiverspress.com

ISBN 978-1-909747-12-8

1 2 3 4 5 6 7 8 9

Two Rivers Press is represented in the UK by Inpress Ltd and
distributed by Central Books.

Cover and text design by Nadja Guggi and typeset in Janson and Parisine

Printed and bound in Great Britain by Imprint Digital, Exeter.

Acknowledgements

All the translations from Rilke, and the prose items in the
appendix, are published here with the permission of the Estate of
Ruth Speirs and that of Special Collections at the University of
Reading, where her archive is preserved. We would like to thank
the staff there for the attentiveness and help they have offered.
We would especially like to thank Guy Baxter, the University
Archivist, for permission to use the detail from a photograph
used on our cover design, a photograph among the Bernard
Spencer papers in Special Collections. Caroline Benson kindly
provided us with the scan used in the design. For their exceptional
combined efforts in tracking down the Jerusalem magazine
Forum, the editors would also like to express grateful thanks to
Claudia Rosenzweig, Gabriel Levin and Anthony Rudolf.

Contents

from *The Book of Hours (1899, 1901, 1903)* | 125

from *Uncollected and Later Poems* (1912–1926) | 139

APPENDIX

Introduction

In the Xmas 1936 issue of *New Verse*, there is a review, probably by the magazine's editor Geoffrey Grigson, of J.B. Leishman's translations of *Sonnets to Orpheus* by Rainer Maria Rilke. It is not a positive review. So negative is it, in fact, that towards its close there comes over the writer a need for some sustained self-justification:

> We have gone on long enough about these worthless translations, because (i) they are translations of a great poet whom English people now could most usefully read *in accurate versions*; (ii) because worthless translations are constantly being passed off on to us without reproof; (iii) because Mr. Leishman has the authority of the Hogarth Press (one of the few firms of a civilized, non-academic, non-big-business nature), and so the authority of Leonard and Virginia Woolf; (iv) because such papers as the *Times Literary Supplement* have blessed these translations; (v) because it has been possible to recommend them with an extract from an adverse review by Mr. Spender in which he said (rather foolishly) that 'it is difficult to praise highly enough the courage, honesty and devotion which have gone to the making of this book.' Do such possessions excuse Mr. Leishman's presumption, stupidity, and inaccuracy?
>
> We have had too much. 'The Duinese Elegies' have already been translated by Edward and Victoria Sackville-West into a version crammed with inaccuracies and ineptitudes; and it is time, surely, that someone so important and so much, we suppose, with a conscience, as Mrs Woolf saw to the immediate stopping of this traffic.

As chance would have it, the review immediately following these trenchant paragraphs, is entitled 'Dylan Thomas' and signed 'C. B. S.'—that's to say, the poet Bernard Spencer, who is gratefully acknowledged in the only separate volume of Rilke translations that Ruth Speirs was able to publish during her lifetime, a *Selected Poems* appearing in wartime Cairo one month after the battle of El Alamein. For it would prove more difficult than the *New Verse* reviewer might have expected both to stop the traffic and to let other vehicles for the understanding of Rilke onto the highway. The Hogarth Press and J.B. Leishman had secured exclusive rights to book publication of translations from this major German-language poet.

Nonetheless, the Ruth Speirs translations of Rilke have long been admired. In his *A History of Western Literature* (1956) the critic, translator, and anthologist J. M. Cohen described them as 'excellent', and a little later, in *Poetry of This Age* (1959), he went as far as to call them 'the best'. On both occasions he was obliged to regret that, for those very copyright reasons, they had never appeared in book form. This overlooked the obscure publication (in some 250 copies) by the Anglo-Egyptian Bookshop, Cairo, in December 1942 of her *Selected Poems* containing sixty-six translations. Yet for all practical purposes Cohen was accurate, for the agreement made by Insel Verlag, Rilke's German publishers, that only the versions by J. B. Leishman for the Hogarth Press would be authorised meant that no other rival volumes would be permitted. This restraint could not be applied to the appearance of individual translations or small selections of poems in journals and magazines. However, until the copyrights expired, every Rilke translator was restricted to such piecemeal enterprises, all of which could be epitomised by the title to Michael Hamburger's *An Unofficial Rilke* (1981), by no means the first to appear from under the embargo, but one of the earliest to be brought out in England—the American copyright situation having long been less draconian in its application.

Yet the publishing situation which J. M. Cohen regretted more than fifty years ago has only now been put right with this Two Rivers Press edition of all Ruth Speirs' surviving translations, making a volume almost twice the size of the elegant, pleasantly plain, *Selected Poems* produced in Cairo at 33, Sharia Kasr el Nil. This appeared, despite the difficulties of wartime publication, in a paperback, glued and stapled, but proving unexpectedly tough, such that most of the few surviving copies, if one is fortunate enough to come across them, remain in surprisingly good condition. Though no publication could hope to match the obscure charisma attaching to that *Selected Poems*, this book is intended to broaden an experience that, until now, has been restricted to only the lucky few able to access one of the surviving copies.

Even more difficult to find than her *Selected Poems*, in the same year Ruth Speirs' debut publications of 'Archaic Torso of Apollo', 'Beloved …', and the fourteenth poem in the first suite of the *Sonnets to Orpheus* appeared in the Cairo magazine *The Citadel*. She remained actively involved in translating Rilke, revising old versions and trying out new ones, until at least the early 1980s, when in her late sixties. Her earliest known acquisitions of Rilke volumes bear the ownership signature 'Ruth Manga Speirs', her married name adopted from the great medievalist John Speirs. Born in Latvia in 1916, she would die in Highgate, North London, in 2000. The following January, their son, Logan, a distinguished professor of English in the USA, donated the archive of his mother's papers through an intermediary to Special Collections at the University of Reading, giving absolute permission for them to be used as the intermediary thought fit. Yet until now these papers have been left largely untouched in two boxes (MS 2492) in Special Collections at the Museum of English Rural Life in Reading.

Rainer Maria Rilke (1875–1926), though in many ways the epitome of what the English tend to think a German writer ought to be, was in fact born in Prague, which, with Vienna and Budapest, formed one of the cardinal cultural reference points in the Austro-Hungary monarchy and empire brought to an end by Sarajevo and the First World War. Having once left Prague, only rarely to return and (as he saw it) not having left early enough, Rilke thereafter lived almost everywhere else: in Russia, Paris, Tuscany, Germany, Denmark and Sweden, on Capri, in Spain, and finally Switzerland—where at Meudon he was to die of a painful leukaemia. The multi-lingualism of Switzerland might be thought to typify the poet's pan-Europeanism, which for him meant not only learning languages, but also writing in some of them, notably French and Russian. Eudo C. Mason's study, *Rilke, Europe and the English-speaking World*, though written previous to the tremendous explosion of translations into English that largely coincides with the lifting of copyright restrictions, covers this territory in an exemplary fashion.

Variously characterized as grand or grandiose, vague, philosophical, abstract, prolix, dour, too pompous for his own good, suffering from what one commentator has called an exacerbated 'continuum of self-examination', Rilke was also multi-generic, writing not only the poems by which he remains best known, but also prose fictions (notably *The Notebooks of Malte Laurids Brigge*), plays, translations (the sonnets of Michelangelo, the *Sonnets from the Portuguese* of Elizabeth Barrett Browning, and the poems of Paul Valéry), verse epistles, thousands upon thousands of letters (more creative endeavours in their own right than 'mere' correspondence), and indeed almost every kind of expressive medium imaginable, anything to which he chose to turn his hand, not always successfully, but always with fervour and application. Living just about anywhere, he was at home nowhere, having never managed his domestic situation (a marriage and a daughter, Ruth) with anything resembling responsibility or imaginative grasp. Squandering, as it seemed to some, all the emotional reserves thereby left untouched largely on *Bildung* and self-development, Rilke translated time into space, travelled, focused like few before him on inanimate objects viewed as correlatives of art, and created a unique corpus of myths on matters as diverse as the 'difficult death', 'intransitive love' (in which he became something of an expert), the youthful dead (one version of himself having metaphorically died in youth), and the poet as *Dichter*—a composite of prophet, preacher, spectator, maker of images, monk, teller of truths, an odd-job man without the least practical skills in his portfolio.

The poetic task could therefore be considered as simultaneously near impossible to accomplish, only to be achieved with difficulty, and yet necessary, essential, much greater than just poetry, though poetic in inspiration. By this means—finding a method only to challenge and supplant it—Rilke generated a creative dynamic frequently frustrated by the very need for utterance which ought in principle to have guaranteed fluency and fluidity, and thereby promoted expressive potential. Rilke suffered, or felt he had in large part inherited, a complex of creative impulses that he found it impossible fully to control. The support of blue-stocking salon women, many of them aristocratic either by birth or bearing, soothed a psyche often in thrall to psychosomatic illness and convalescence, unusual, unpredictable or even eccentric behaviour, and an irremovable commitment to separateness. Rilke attributed his doctrine of work to lessons learned during his brief employ as a secretary to the great sculptor Rodin, and the work that emerged from his complexes and contradictions could be thought a justification for their excessiveness. Yet at his best Rilke was as incomparable as he supposed himself to be, and there are more 'classic' poems in his oeuvre than that of any other poet writing in German during the twentieth century.

What Ruth Speirs thought of Rilke as a man, notably his 'foibles and absurdities', can be read and coolly assessed in the yellowing pages of the *Times Literary Supplement* in its unsigned heyday. Like many literary figures revered in their own day (James Joyce, T. S. Eliot, Virginia Woolf), Rilke was not often likeable in the ways we for the most part prefer our friends to be. But Speirs was not a person given to wide-eyed devotion, and in any case her interest was the poetry, and of Rilke's great value as a poet she was never in doubt. No one able to read, or to read some of, this poet in the original can be in any uncertainty that they have had an extraordinary experience. Ruth attempted, with the best of motives, to make the extraordinary a little less forbidding, where it proved possible to do so. In the typically modest, plain manner of her preface for the Cairo *Selected Poems*—which could not fit better the appearance of the book it introduces—she writes: 'What I have aimed at is to give as exact a translation of Rilke as is humanly possible.'

The keyword here is 'humanly', something the poet aimed at but could not always be said to have achieved. Studious as Rilke was of a difficult simplicity, Ruth had no option, by virtue of her striving to be 'exact', but to leave something of that strangeness and estrangement as an intrinsic part of her translations. When Rilke spoke (in the poem 'Apparition', in her version of it) of 'the other side of the voice', he was aware of his own sometimes self-defeating tendency to write

5

in a manner uniquely his own. He sounds just as unique to a German ear as he is bound to seem to an English one. Only in re-reading him can he be brought into some kind of adequate focus. But no one did more, or worked harder, than Ruth Speirs to make Rilke sound as if he might just possibly have written originally in English—one of the few major languages he read 'only with difficulty', as Ruth Speirs put it in the *TLS* for 28 July 1961.

Consider her opening to the seventeenth poem in the second suite of *Sonnets to Orpheus* as published here:

> Where, in what ever blissfully watered gardens, on what trees, out of what calyxes tenderly stripped of their petals, do they ripen, the strange fruits of consolation?

In *Reading Rilke: Reflections on the Problems of Translation* (1999), William H. Gass has the following to say of a version, revised from the text in her 1942 *Selected Poems*, that Angel Flores printed in *An Anthology of German Poetry from Hölderlin to Rilke* (1960): 'Where, in whichever blissfully watered gardens, on which / Trees, and out of which tenderly unpetaled flower cups / Do they ripen, the strange fruits of consolation?' Gass writes that 'Spiers [sic] replaces the word "what" with the word "which"—why? However, her "unpetaled flower cups" seems the most natural and least forced.' She will never have read these words, but in the further revised text we print it is as if Speirs had responded to his question by altering each 'which' to a 'what'—and, more, she has returned to what Gass praises as 'most natural and least forced' so as to remove the neologism 'unpetaled', adopt the appropriate term 'calyxes' for the poetical 'flower cups', and choose the participle 'stripped' to express the action of having its petals removed. If we then compare this with Rilke's original ('aus welchen zärtlich entblätterten Blüten-Kelchen'), we can see that her 'unpetaled' is an attempt at his 'entblätterten' (which might be 'unleafed', from 'blätte'—leaves), while 'stripped' comes to her from a verb commonly used to describes what happens to trees in autumn. 'Kelchen' are calyxes and 'zärtlich' is tender. So for the loss of 'Blüten' (flowers), which can be understood from the context, we end up with 'out of what calyxes tenderly stripped of their petals'—a rhythmically alive phrase which accurately renders the original and is even more 'natural' and less 'forced' than the version Gass praised.

Comparing it with the phrase in the 2011 Oxford World's Classics *Selected Poems* reveals another problem that Speirs avoids. That version, by Susan Ransom and Marielle Sutherland, reads 'developed from which petal cups tenderly peeled'. The participle 'peeled', as of an apple, is there to rhyme with 'field' in the fourth line of this opening quatrain, and could be said to respond to Rilke's form, though he rhymes his first two lines 'welchen / Kelchen', so his AABB pattern is not perfectly imitated. With her ambition 'to give as exact a translation of Rilke as is humanly possible', Speirs could not compromise sense for rhyme, and yet when it arose she would accommodate it as best she could, as for example here in her 'Blue Hydrangea':

> Like green left over in a pot of paint,
> the leaves look dry and lustreless and rough
> behind the clustered blooms that have no blue
> but merely mirror it from far away.
>
> Their mirroring seems blurred with tears, and vague
> as though they were to lose it soon again;
> as in blue writing-paper faded with the years
> there is some yellow in them, mauve and grey;
>
> a washed-out colour as in children's pinafores,
> no longer worn, with nothing to befall it now:
> how it conveys to us a small life's brevity!
>
> But suddenly the blueness seems renewed
> within one of the clusters, and we see
> a touching blue rejoice before the green.

Rilke's sonnet has ABBA rhymes in its first two quatrains, with the B rhyme-sounds in the first verse becoming the A ones in the second. Speirs has not attempted to reproduce this formal feature. Yet just as the 'blau' (blue) of Rilke's line three is echoed in the 'Grau' (grey) of his eighth, so Speirs is able to echo her 'away' in line four with 'grey' in line eight, and where she cannot end-rhyme, as here, the opportunity for an internal rhyme 'tears' in line five with 'years' at the end of line seven emerges, she will accept it. Similarly, in the final three lines of the sonnet, though Rilke rhymes his final and antepenultimate lines, she enables the near-rhyming couplet of 'see' and 'green' to give her version a sense of the closure appropriate to sonnets in English. So again, Ruth Speirs provides a rendering that is 'natural' and not 'forced', yet which throughout has effective rhythm and occasionally some rhyme where the English makes it possible.

It is a privilege and a pleasure thus finally to pay Ruth Speirs belated homage, much too late for comfort but better late than never: homage to an exceptionally gifted translator of a great European figure, homage of the kind she was pleased and relieved to receive in her lifetime from poets and poet-critics such as William Empson, Bernard Spencer, Terence Tiller, Ian Fletcher, G. S. Fraser, Francis Berry, Michael Hamburger, Nicholas Moore, Herbert Read, E. V. Rieu and many more, as well as from such writers and commentators as C. M. Bowra, Cyril Connolly, John Hayward, D. W. Harding, V. S. Pritchett, Ernst Stahl, and Stanley Edgar Hyman, and from such admirable editors as Angel Flores in *An Anthology of German Poetry from Hölderlin to Rilke* (1960) and Willis Barnstone in *Modern European Poetry* (1966). Speirs contributed to six or seven anthologies of varying merit, sometimes (as with *Springtime*, published by *Poetry London* in 1953) earning accolades when most of the other contributions were dismissed as dross. None of these excursions were the Rilke of Ruth Speirs in their own book, because that could not be; but they were *in* books, and so less ephemeral than the journals and magazines (*Personal Landscape*, *Poetry London*, *The New Statesman and Nation*, *Nine*, *Arena*, *The Listener*) where her versions first appeared.

There is now perhaps more Rilke available in English than even the poet himself would have been able to come to terms with or write about at length in letters, the diametric opposite of the copyright situation which made Leishman's voice the only one most people could ever hear. His name would often wittily, if understandably caustically, appear on Ruth Speirs' lips as *Leichnam* ('corpse' in German). Other opinions of Leishman—an excellent critic and teacher—as a translator were even less printable, and remain in the private correspondence between Leonard Woolf and Stephen Spender, Leishman's often uncomfortable collaborator on the *Duino Elegies* venture between late 1937 and spring 1939, which can be found in Nadja Guggi's admirable and unpublished dissertation on these and kindred matters. It is relatively rare for any translator not attempting completeness in bringing over a poet into his or her own language (in Speirs' case she was working with her second and third) to attempt in excess of one hundred versions. Even the indefatigable Leishman over more than forty years, utterly committed to an exceptionally prolific poet, could not encompass everything, his extraordinarily wide sweep, 'the sheer industry and concentration' noted by Speirs in a *TLS* review of *Poems* 1906–26, which 'commands respect', notwithstanding. Her total of almost one hundred and twenty poems is more than respectable, but probably less than might have resulted if publishing conditions had been favourable, and if she had not such exercised control over what was in her view worth working on.

Ruth Speirs' Rilke fell under the repression of '[a] sort of mortmain', as her friend and fellow-poet Terence Tiller once aptly put it in a letter written a few months before he died (UoR MS 2492, Box Two). Yet rather than on a dead hand, or on the dead hand of more than one translator, it is no doubt better to end on the note struck by Lawrence Durrell in a newspaper (*The Egyptian Gazette*) review of January 1943, less than a month after the publication of the *Selected Poems* by the Anglo-European Bookshop. Durrell considered them 'lucid and pure as water', and wrote of this Rilke as having been 'literally born into English'. He hoped, rather too sanguinely, that Ruth's versions would perhaps 'become the definitive translations of this rare and singular German poet'. They do not any longer, if indeed they ever did, need to be 'definitive', but they do, as Durrell was probably the first to point out, deserve to be read. '*Here*', as she so memorably renders it in the ninth of the *Duino Elegies*, 'is the Sayable, *here* is its home.'

John Pilling & Peter Robinson

Editors' Note

We have organized our complete edition of the surviving translations that Ruth Speirs made from the poetry of Rainer Maria Rilke into two parts. The first contains, in order of original publication, her renderings from the triptych of the poet's major achievement: *Die Neue Gedichte* (New Poems), *Duineser Elegien* (Duino Elegies), and *Die Sonnette an Orpheus* (Sonnets to Orpheus). She offers us a complete version of the central panel, and substantial selections from the flanking wings. Our second part brings together her shorter selections from Rilke's early collections, and those from the large volume of his later uncollected poems. Readers wishing to experience something of the chronological development of the poet's art can easily do so by reading the first two sections of our part two, followed by the whole of part one, concluding with the final section in part two of later uncollected work.

In the Ruth Speirs papers at the University of Reading are some—there must once have been several more—of the Rilke books which she owned and from which she worked, notably *Das Stunden-Buch* (The Book of Hours, her copy bearing the inscription 'Kairo 1939'), her 1930 Insel-Verlag Leipzig *Neue Gedichte* (New Poems, purchased 1940), *Das Buch der Bilder* (The Book of Images, purchased in Haifa in early 1942), and the second of two volumes of selections published in Germany (Insel-Verlag, 1936) after Rilke's death. From these it can be seen that, when and where Ruth had made a translation, she indicates as much, either by writing in pencil at the end of the poem 'RMS', or in contents pages checking items in the margin, or underlining (in ink), or drawing a line through, individual titles. It seems safe on this basis to assume that she must at one time or another have worked on about a dozen of the poems in *Das Stunden-Buch* (only eight versions now survive, not including any versions of the poems she numbered 13, 14, 15, 31 and 32), and on roughly the same number from *Das Buch der Bilder* (there are now only nine of these).

Titles checked in the Insel selection (their second volume, with the signature 'Ruth Manga Speirs Cairo 1939') suggest there may once have been versions of 'Der Schauende' (The Spectator) [from The Book of Images], 'Klage' (Lament) [from the Uncollected later and last poems 1906–1926], 'Fünf Gesänge' (Five Songs) [ditto], 'Der Goldschmied' (The Goldsmith) [ditto], 'Himmelfahrt Mariae I and II' [but not III] (The Assumption of Mary into Heaven) [from *Das Marienleben* / The Life of Mary], 'Zu de Zeichnung, John Keats …' (On a deathbed drawing of John Keats) [ditto], 'O sage Dichter, was du tust …' ('Tell us Poet, what it is you do …') [ditto]. We would very much have liked to publish all of these for the first time here, alongside the other *inédits* that appear in this collection; but there are no texts to be found in her archive. Also lost, but on lists compiled by Ruth, is 'So strained against strong night …' from the uncollected later poems (the original poem opens '*So angestrengt wider die starke Nacht …*').

Readers can find at the end of the Notes a checklist of versions that are either lost, 'dropped' (her way of indicating not just items which for one reason or another were submitted to magazines but never appeared, but also poems jettisoned or abandoned with all faults—we have reprinted the latter where they are extant), or otherwise seemingly irretrievable. Though the Jerusalem journal *Forum* published by the Palestine Broadcasting Company in pre-Israel days has surfaced, similar searches for the Cairo magazine *The Citadel* edited by David Hicks in 1942 and 1943 having unfortunately proved unavailing.

John Pilling & Peter Robinson,
April 2015

PART I

from *New Poems*

ONE (1907)

Abishag

I

She lay. Her arms, a child's, were tied
by servants round the faded man
on whom she lay for sweet long hours,
a little fearful of his many years.

And when an owl screeched, now and then,
she turned her face round in his beard;
and everything that was the night, drew near
with fear and longing, to surround her.

As though akin to her, stars trembled,
a fragrance searched the sleeping-chamber,
the curtain stirred and gave a sign,
the sign was softly followed by her gaze.

But she held on to him, the dark old man,
and by the night of nights not reached
she lay as royal blood grew chill beneath her,
virginal, weightless like a soul.

II

The king sat thinking of the empty day
of deeds performed, desires he had not felt,
and of his favourite hound he lavished care on.
But in the evening, Abishag
curved over him. His tangled life
lay like a coast of ill repute deserted
beneath the constellation of her quiet breasts.

And sometimes, knowing much of women,
he recognised from underneath his brows
the unmoved mouth that held no kisses,
and realised: the green twig of her feelings
did not bend down towards his depth.
He shivered. Listened like a dog,
and sought himself in his last blood.

The Departure of the Prodigal Son

Now to depart from all that is entangled
and that is ours and yet is not our own,
that tremblingly reflects us, like the water
in old wells, and destroys our image;
from all this which, as though with thorns,
is once more clinging to us—to depart,
and suddenly to look
at This and Him one had no longer seen
(they were so daily and so ordinary):
with gentleness, in reconciliation
to understand—as if at a beginning,
close up, and apprehending—how impersonally,
how over and above us all that suffering happened
of which our childhood had been full up to the brim—:
yet to depart, hand out of hand,
as if one tore again what was already healed,
and to depart: where? Into the uncertain,
far into some warm unrelated land
indifferent behind all action
like backcloth: garden, or a wall;
and to depart: why? Out of impulse, one's own nature,
impatience, dark expectancy, and out of
not being understood and one's not understanding.

To take all this upon oneself and drop
in vain what one perhaps had held,
to die alone, not knowing why—

Is that the entrance into a new life?

The Cathedral

In those small towns in which old houses
squat round about it like a fair
that suddenly and frightened, having noticed it,
shuts up the booths and, closed and mute

the criers silent and the drums arrested,
is listening up to it excitedly, all ear,
while in the old full mantle of its counterforts
it placidly stands always there

and has no knowledge of the houses:
in those small towns, you see
to what extent cathedrals had outgrown

all else. Their rise passed beyond everything,
as vision is continually outstripped
by far too great preoccupation with one's life

as though, beside it, nothing happened;
and as if fate were limitless accumulation,
turned into stone in them, and meant to last,
and were not that which in dark streets below

picks up by chance some name or other
and walks about in it, as children wear green, red
and anything the dealer has, as pinafores.
In those foundations there was birth,

and strength and thrust were in that towering,
and love was everywhere like bread and wine,
and portals harboured love's laments.

Life hesitated in the striking of the hours,
and in the towers which in renunciation
quite suddenly no longer rose, was Death.

The Portal

There they remained as if the flood
whose great surge washed against these stones
till they took shape, had now retreated;
subsiding, it had taken various attributes

out of their hands which are too kind
and generous to be holding on to anything.
There they remained, from basalt forms
distinguishable by a nimbus,

a mitre, sometimes by a smile
for which a face retained the peace
of former hours to serve as quiet dial;

confined now to their portal's emptiness,
they once had been the ear
which caught this city's every moan.

II

A wide expanse is here implied:
as scenic wings imply the world
and as through those there steps the hero
wrapped in the cloak of his performance:

the darkness of the portal, acting,
steps on the tragic stage of its own depth,
as infinite and changeful as is God the Father,
like Him, assuming wondrous transformation

into a Son, dispersed here over many
small, almost silent roles
adopted from the range of misery.

For only thus (we know) there still arises
from those cast out, insane, and blind
the Saviour as the only actor.

The Rose Window

In there: the lazy pacing of their paws
creates an almost disconcerting silence;
as, all at once, one of the cats
takes forcibly in its great eye

the straying glance that plays across it,—
the glance which, seized as by a whirlpool,
keeps swimming for a little while,
to sink, no longer conscious of itself,

when, seemingly at rest, this eye springs open
and closes over it as with a torrent's roar
and sweeps it headlong down into red blood:

thus, in past ages, from the dark
the great rose windows of cathedrals seized
a heart and swept it headlong into God.

The Capital

Thus as from the abortions of a dream,
ascending from confounding torture,
the next day rises,—the vault's girths
go forth from the chaotic capital,

and they leave creatures in it, flapping wings,
compactly and mysteriously entwined:
their hesitation, the heads' suddenness
and those strong leaves the sap of which

rises like sudden fury, finally capsizing
in a swift gesture clenching to a fist
and holding itself out: and chasing upwards

all that always again falls downwards, cold,
with darkness, and—like rain—provides
the maintenance of this old growth.

God in the Middle Ages

They had saved him up within themselves
and they wanted him to *be* and judge,
And at last attached to him like weights,
(to prevent his rise to Heaven)

their large cathedrals' mass and burden.
And above his boundless numbers
he was, pointing, merely to revolve
and to give direction like a clock

to their actions and their daily tasks.
But all at once he started moving fully,
and the people of the terror-stricken town,

frightened with his voice, allowed him
to go on, his clock-work all unhinged,
and fled before the dial.

The Prisoner

I

My hand has only one gesture
with which it scares away;
something keeps falling, damp,
from rocks, on the old stones.

I hear only this knocking,
my heart is keeping time
with the going of the drops
and with it, fades away.

If only they dripped faster,
if an animal came again.
Somewhere there was more light—.
But we, what do we know.

II

Imagine that, what now is sky and wind,
air for your mouth and brightness for your eyes,
turned into stone up to the little space
on which your hands are and your heart;

and that what now, in you, is called tomorrow
and: then, and: later-on, the coming year, and farther—
grew sore within you and was full of pus
and only festered and broke no more open;

and that, what was, became insane
and raved within you, your dear mouth
—that never laughed—with laughter foaming;

and that, what God was, only was your gaoler
and stuffed, malignant, into the last hole
a dirty eye. And yet you lived.

The Panther

Jardin des Plantes, Paris

His gaze has grown so weary of the passing
of bars that there is nothing it retains.
It seems to him there are a thousand bars
and out beyond a thousand bars no world.

The fluid motion of his supple, powerful paces
revolving in the very smallest circle
is like a dance of strength around a centre
in which there stands, stunned, a great will.

Only at times the curtain of the pupil
glides open without sound—. An image enters,
moves through the concentrated stillness of his limbs—
and in his heart it ceases to exist.

A Woman's Fate

The way a king, out hunting, seized a glass
haphazardly, to drink from, and its owner
set it aside and kept it safely stored
as though it were no ordinary thing:

Fate, also thirsty, raised from time to time
a woman to his lips, and drank her
whom then a narrow life, too much afraid
of breaking her, kept safe from any use

and set her down inside the fragile glass case
in which there are its various treasures
(or objects that are looked upon as precious).

A stranger, there she stood, as though on loan
and she grew merely old and she grew blind
and was not precious and was never rare.

The Convalescent

The way a singing comes and goes in streets,
now approaches, now again shrinks back,
flutters, almost grasped at times,
then again dispersed and far away:

Life is playing with the convalescent
while she, drained of strength, and rested,
awkwardly, to yield to it,
makes an unaccustomed gesture.

And she feels it almost as seduction
when her hardened hand which held
fevers full of contradictions
comes from far, as with a blossoming
touch to fondle her hard chin.

The Grown-Up

It all stood there on her and was the world
and stood on her with all things, fear and mercy,
as trees stand, growing and erect, entirely image
and imageless as is the Ark of the Covenant,
and solemn as if placed upon a people.

And she bore up to it; bore to the brim
the flying, fleeing, far-away, immense
and not yet learned,—serenely like a water-bearer
her full jar. Till in the midst of playing
the first white veil, transforming, and preparing
for something else, fell softly gliding
across the new awareness in her face,

almost opaque, and never rose again
and somehow gave to all her questions
the one reiterated vague reply:
In you yourself, you once-a-child, in you.

Parting

How I have felt what parting means! How well
I know it still: dark, cruel, never overcome,
it gives awareness of a perfect union,
and holds it out, and tears it all apart.

And how defenceless I was, watching
what, calling to me, let me go
and stayed behind as though it were all women,
yet small and white and nothing more than this:

a waving which applied to me no longer,
a slight continued waving—, and already
barely explainable: maybe a plum-tree
from which a cuckoo rose in hasty flight.

Experience of Death

Nothing is known to us about this passing;
it does not let us share. We have no cause
for showing admiration, love, or hate
to Death disfigured strangely by a tragic

mask's lamenting mouth. As yet,
the world is full of parts for us to play.
As long as we concern ourselves with pleasing,
Death, though displeasing, also acts a part.

But, as you went, a glimpse of realness
flashed in upon our stage by that same crevice
through which you passed: the green of real verdure,
the real sunshine, and the real wood.

We go on acting, and reciting lines
learnt anxiously and with a painful effort,
and now and then we raise our hands, and gesture;
but your existence, far from us, removed

out of our play, can sometimes come upon us
like knowledge of that realness—
and we are acting Life a little while,
carried away, not thinking of applause.

Blue Hydrangea

Like green left over in a pot of paint,
the leaves look dry and lustreless and rough
behind the clustered blooms that have no blue
but merely mirror it from far away.

Their mirroring seems blurred with tears, and vague
as though they were to lose it soon again;
as in blue writing-paper faded with the years
there is some yellow in them, mauve and grey;

a washed-out colour as in children's pinafores,
no longer worn, with nothing to befall it now:
how it conveys to us a small life's brevity!

But suddenly the blueness seems renewed
within one of the clusters, and we see
a touching blue rejoice before the green.

The Steps of the Orangerie

Versailles

Like kings who ultimately, almost aimless,
wrapped in the loneliness of royal robes,
only stride forth to show themselves at times
to those who bow to them at either side:—

thus mounts, alone, between the balustrades
which have been bowing since the first beginnings,
the flight of steps here: slowly, by the grace of God,
and heavenwards, and not to anywhere;

as if it had commanded all attendants
to stay behind, so that they dare not follow—
not even at a distance; and not one
has been allowed to bear the heavy train.

The Merry-Go-Round

Jardin du Luxembourg

With roof and shadow, multi-coloured horses
go round and round a little while;
they all are of the land that lingers
before at last it vanishes away.
Though some are harnessed to a carriage
their countenances all convey their daring;
a fierce red lion goes along with them,
and now and then an elephant, a white one.

There even is a stag which looks exactly
like those in forests, but it bears a saddle
and, firmly strapped, a little girl in blue.

And on the lion rides a boy in white
and grips him tightly with a small hot hand,
the lion meanwhile showing teeth and tongue.

And now and then an elephant, a white one.

Astride the horses, they pass by; among them,
young girls who almost have outgrown
the plunging of such steeds; while swinging by,
they raise their glance, across to here, to somewhere—

And now and then an elephant, a white one.

And on it goes and hurries to an end,
revolves and turns and has no aim.
A red, a green, a grey is carried past,
a little profile barely yet begun,
from time to time a smile that strays this way,
a blissful smile that dazzles and is lavished
upon this blind and breathless sport.

Spanish Dancer

As in one's hand a sulphur-match,
white, before blazing, darts in all directions
convulsive tongues: her round dance starts,
precipitate, bright, hot, to spread convulsively
within the narrow circle of spectators.

All of a sudden it is all ablaze.

And with a glance she sets her hair alight
and, suddenly, with daring art, she whirls
her whole attire into this conflagration
from which there reach like frightened snakes
her bare arms, rattling, wide awake.

And then: as if the fire were tightening about her,
she gathers it together, flings it off
very imperiously and with a haughty gesture,
and gazes: raging, there it lies,
refusing to surrender, still a blaze.
But sure, triumphant, with a sweet
saluting smile, she lifts her face,—
and stamps it out with small firm feet.

The Square

Furnes

Widened by the impact of events long past:
by rage and riot, by the motley crowd
escorting men condemned to death,
by booths, the shouts of criers at the fair,
the Duke on horseback, riding by,
Burgundian arrogance and pride,

(enclosed by background on all sides):

the square incessantly invites the distant windows
to enter its expanse—while, slowly, the attendants
and followers of emptiness proceed
to group themselves along the rows of stalls.

The little houses, climbing into gables,
insist on seeing everything, and shyly
they keep the towers secret from each other:
the boundless presence ever at their backs.

The Island

North Sea

I

The flood to come will level out the path
there in the shallows, everything around
will be alike; but yonder little island
has closed its eyes; the dyke revolves,

bewildering, around its dwellers who are born
into a sleep in which they mutely intermingle
many worlds; they rarely speak,
each of their sentences is like an epitaph

for something that is washed up on their shore
and unfamiliar, coming unexplained to them
and staying. Everything their gaze describes

has been like that since childhood: not applied to them,
too great, and inconsiderate, and sent this way,
exaggerating their own loneliness still more.

II

As if it lay within a crater's ring
upon a moon: each farmstead has a dyke
around it, and the gardens inside are
all dressed the same, and combed the same

like orphans, by that storm which so severely rears them
and frightens them for days with death.
Then people sit inside the houses
and see in slanting mirrors what strange things

are standing on the chests-of-drawers. In the evening
one of the sons steps out before the door
and draws a tune from the accordion, as soft as weeping;

thus he had heard it in a foreign harbour—.
And on the outer dyke, one of the sheep adopts
very large outlines and is almost threatening.

III

Only what is within is near; all else is distant.
And this within is thronged and every day filled over-full
with everything, and quite untellable. The island
is like too small a star

which space does not perceive and silently destroys
in its unconscious formidableness,
so that the star, un-lit, un-heard,
alone,

(that all this should come to an end)
tries moving, dark, upon a self-invented course,
blindly, and not within the scheme
of planets, suns and systems.

Orpheus. Eurydice. Hermes

It was the strange mine of the souls.
They went like veins of silent silver-ore
throughout its darkness. Between roots
there sprang the blood that goes forth to mankind,
heavy like porphyry in all that darkness.
Else there was nothing red.

Rocks were there
and unsubstantial forests. Bridges over void
and that large grey blind pond
which hung above the ground beneath its depth
like rainy skies above a landscape.
And between meadows, gentle and full of forbearance,
appeared the pale strip of that single path
like linen spread in a long row to bleach.

Along that single path they came.

Taking the lead, the slender blue-cloaked man
impatiently looked straight ahead, in silence;
and, in large bites, his steps devoured the path
—not even chewing—while his hands hung heavy
and clenched out of the fall of folds,
no longer conscious of the lyre
grown lightly into his left hand as tendrils
of roses grow into an olive branch.
His senses were in discord:
his gaze ran, like a dog, ahead,
turned round, came back, and always stood far-off
and waited by a turning of the path—
his hearing, like a scent, remained behind.
It seemed to him at times as though it reached
back to the footfall of those two
who were to follow him in this ascent.
And then again, behind him, there was only
the echo of his climb, the air stirred by his cloak.
But he assured himself that they were coming,
said it aloud and heard the sound subside;
that they were coming, only they were two

who stepped extremely softly. If he were allowed
to turn but once (if looking back were not
entire undoing of this deed still in the process
of being done) he then would see those two
who, moving softly, follow him in silence:

the god of movement and of distant message,
his light eyes shaded by the travelling-hood,
bearing the slender staff before him,
and fluttering wings about his feet;
and given to his left hand: *she*.

She, so beloved that more lament
came from a lyre than wails from wailing-women;
that, from lament, a world arose
in which there were all things once more: wood, dale,
path, hamlet, river, field, and beast;
and that round this lament-world, as around
the other earth, there was a sun
revolving and a quiet starry sky,
lament-sky with distorted stars—:
she, so beloved.

Led by the god's hand, she was walking,
her step constricted by the dead's long linen bands,
unsteady, gentle and without impatience.
She was within herself like one full of high hope,
not thinking of the man who went ahead,
not of the path that rose up into life.
She was within herself. Her having died
filled her like fullness.
And as a fruit is filled with sweetness and the dark,
thus she was full of her great death
which was so new that she grasped nothing.
She was in a new maidenhood,
untouchable; her sex was closed
like a young flower towards the evening,
and so much had her hands grown disaccustomed
to wedlock that the infinitely gentle
touch of the light god as he guided her
offended her like too great intimacy.

She was no more that fair-haired woman
who sometimes echoed in the poets' songs,
no more the broad bed's scent and island,
and that man's property no more.
She was already loosened like long hair,
given away like falling rain,
distributed like hundredfold provision.

She was already root.
And when, all of a sudden,
the god abruptly stopped her and, his exclamation
full of pain, he spoke the words: He has turned round—,
she comprehended nothing and said softly: Who?

But in the distance, dark against the clear way out,
stood somebody whose face
could not be recognised. He stood and saw
how on a strip of meadow-path
the god of message, sadness in his gaze, was turning silently to follow
the form already going back by that same path,
her step constricted by the dead's long linen bands,
unsteady, gentle, and without impatience.

Alcestis

The messenger was suddenly among them,
flung like a new ingredient
into the boiling-over of the wedding feast.
They drank, and were not conscious of the god
who entered secretly and held his godship
close to his body like a sodden cloak
and who, as he went past, appeared to be
someone or other, one of them.
But suddenly, while in the midst of speaking,
one of the guests saw the young host,
there at the table's upper end, jerk upwards
from his recumbent attitude, reflecting
—all of him, his very being—something strange
that terribly addressed itself to him.
As though the mixture clarified there was
immediate silence; underneath, a sediment
of turbid noise and a precipitate of falling babble
with a decaying smell of dull stale laughter.
And there they recognised the slender god;
and as he stood there, full of purpose and inexorable—
they almost knew. And yet, when it was said, it was
more than all knowledge and impossible to grasp.
Admetus is to die. When? In this hour.

But he broke off his horror's shell
in pieces; out of it he stretched
his hands to bargain with the god.
For years, for still one single year of youth,
for months, for weeks, a few more days,
not days, ah, nights, for only one,
for one night, only for this *one*: for *this* one.
The god refused; and there he screamed
and screamed it out and did not hold it back and screamed
as, giving birth, his mother had screamed out.

And, an old woman, she came up to him,
the father, the old father, came; and both
stood—helpless, old and obsolete—beside him
who screamed; but suddenly he scrutinized them closely
as never once before, broke off, and swallowed, said:
Father,
do you much value this remainder,
this sediment, that hinders you devouring?
Go, pour it out. And you, old woman,
matron,
what are you doing here still: you have given birth.
He held them both like beasts of sacrifice
within one grip. And suddenly released them,
thrust them aside, inspired and radiant,
drew breath, and called out: Kreon, Kreon!
And nothing else; and nothing but this name.
But in his face was what he did not say,
unutterably full of expectation,
as, in a glow, he held it out to his young friend,
his dearest friend, across the littered table.
Old people (said his face) can be no ransom
for they are spent and bad and almost worthless
but you, in all your beauty, you—

But then he saw his friend no more
who fell behind; and who approached was *she*,
a little smaller, almost, than he knew her,
and frail and sad in her pale wedding-gown.
And all the rest are nothing but the lane
through which she keeps approaching—: (now
she will be in his aching open arms).
But as he waits she speaks; but not to him.
Speaks to the god, the god notes what she says,
and they all hear it only as if in the god:

Nobody else can take his place but I can.
I take his place. No one has reached the end
as I have. What is left to me
of what I have been here? Indeed, I die.
Did she, who sent you on this mission,
not tell you that the bed which waits in there
is of the Underworld? I bade farewell.
Farewell upon farewell.
No one who dies bids more farewell. I left
and everything was to dissolve and vanish
buried beneath him who is now my husband—.
Take me away: I die for him.

And, as the wind on high seas swiftly changes
its course, the god approached her, almost
as if she were already dead—
and suddenly far off from her husband
to whom he flung, concealed in a small gesture,
the hundred lives of this earth. Reeling,
he rushed towards them and reached out
to grasp them, as if in a dream. Already
they neared the entrance where, in tears,
the women thronged. But still once more he saw
the face she turned back with a radiant smile
of hope which almost was a promise:
grown-up, to come back from deep death to him
who lived—

            And suddenly, upon his knees, he thrust
his hands up to his face, that after
this smile he should see nothing more.

The Birth of Venus

That morning—following the night which, full of fear
had passed with cries, disquiet, tumult—
the sea once more burst open, screamed.
And when the scream had slowly closed again,
and fell into the abyss of dumb fishes,
down from the pale day and beginning of the skies—:
the sea gave birth.

With the first sun there gleamed the hair-foam
of the wide groin of billows at whose brim
the maiden, white, embarrassed, wet, arose.
And as a young green leaf stirs, stretches
and gradually unfolds its rolled-up borders,
her body opened to the coolness
and to the untouched early wind.

The knees rose clear like moons
and dived into the cloudy borders of the thighs;
the slender shadow of the calves retreated,
the feet became elastic and grew bright,
alive like throats of people drinking
were the joints.

In the cup of the pelvis lay the belly
like a young fruit in a child's hand.
Within its navel's narrow goblet
was the whole darkness of this luminous life.
Below it, gleaming, rose the little wave
constantly overflowing towards the loins
where now and then there was a quiet purling.
But full of light and without shadows yet
—as is a birch-tree grove in April—
warm, empty and unhidden lay the sex.

And now the brisk scales of the shoulders stood
in equipoise already on the upright body
that rose out of the pelvis like a fountain
and, hesitating, fell in the long arms
and, swifter, in the full fall of the hair.

And then the face passed very slowly by:
from the foreshortened darkness of its bending
to clear horizontal rise.
Behind it, steep, the chin closed in.

Now that the neck was straightened like a sunbeam
and like a flower-stem in which sap rises,
the arms stretched forward too, like necks
of swans when searching for the shore.

And the first draw of breath then came
like morning wind into this body's early dawn.
In the most tender branches of the vein-trees
a whisper rose, the blood began
to rush above its depths.
This wind increased: and into the new breasts
it flung itself with all its breath
and filled them and pressed into them,
so that they drove—sails full of distance—
the weightless maiden towards the shore.

And thus the goddess landed.

Behind her,
who strode hurriedly along young shores,
the whole forenoon
flowers and blades of grass rose, warm, embarrassed,
as if out of embrace. She went, she ran.

But in the hardest hour, at noon,
the sea rose once again and flung
a dolphin onto the same spot.
Dead, red, and open.

TWO (1908)

Archaic Torso of Apollo

We have not known his incredible head
in which the flowers of his eyes grew to maturing. But
his torso still glimmers like a chandelier
in which his gaze, whose light is merely lowered,

holds fast and glows. If it were otherwise,
his chest's prow could not blind you, and a smile
could not be moving in the gentle turning of his loins
up to that centre which had borne the sex.

If it were otherwise, this stone would stand
short and distorted under the transparent fall of shoulders
and would not glisten like the skin of beasts of prey

and would not, like a star, burst out
of all its rims; there is no spot
that does not see you. You must change your life.

The Death of the Beloved

He knew of death no more than what we all know:
it takes and thrusts us into what is mute.
But when, not torn away from him,
no, gently loosened from his eyes,

she glided past to unknown shadows,
and when he felt they had their maiden smile
now yonder like a moon
and their own way of doing good:

the dead grew as well known to him
as if through her he were quite closely
related to each one of them; he let the others speak,

did not believe, and called that land
the ever-sweet and the well-situated—.
And with his touch prepared it for her feet.

A Sibyl

Once, long ago, they called her old.
But she lived on and wandered every day
along the self-same street. They changed
the measures—like a forest's age

hers now was told by centuries. But she
came every evening to the self-same spot
where, high and hollow and burnt out,
black like an ancient citadel, she stood

while the words that multiplied unguarded
and against her will in her
screamed and flew incessantly about her,

with the ones that had returned
sitting, dark, beneath her brows,
ready for the night.

The Insane in the Garden

Dijon

The old Carthusian cloisters still enclose
the courtyard as if something healed in there.
Those, too, who now inhabit them make pause
and take no part in life outside.

Things which *could* happen came and passed away.
And now they like to walk familiar paths,
and part, and come to meet each other,
describing circles, willing, primitive.

Some cultivate the flower-beds of spring,
indigent, humble, down upon their knees;
but when nobody sees it
they have a furtive, twisted

gesture for the tender early grass,
a testing, timid fondling:
the grass is friendly, while the red roses
might be excess again, and threaten them,

and might perhaps again transcend
what, in their souls, they recognize and know.
But this can still be kept a secret;
how good the grass is and how quiet.

Unknown Family

As dust, which somehow comes into existence
and which is nowhere, for a purpose unexplained
hurriedly curdles into grey some empty morning
in a corner where one casts a glance,—

there they took shape, who knows of what,
the very moment you were drawing close,
amid the sodden debris of the street
they were an indeterminable something

that was concerned with you. Or not with you.
A voice, as though last year's, sang out
to you and yet remained a weeping;
a hand, as though on loan, came forward
and yet it did not grasp your own.
Who is to come? Whom have these four in mind?

Washing the Corpse

They had got used to him. But when
the kitchen lamp was brought, restlessly burning
in the dark draught of air, the unknown man
was quite unknown. They washed his neck,

and as they had no knowledge of his fate
they pieced another one together with their lies,
while washing all the time. The one
began to cough, the heavy sponge of vinegar

left lying on his face. The other also paused.
From their hard brush, the drops fell, knocking,
While his horrible contorted hand
wanted to prove to all the house
he was no longer thirsty.

And he did prove. As though embarrassed,
and with a hurried cough, the women hastened
to recommence their work, their crooked shadows
writhing and twisting in the silent pattern

on papered walls, as if inside a net,
till they who washed had done.
In the uncurtained window-frame
night was relentless. One without a name
lay clean and naked there, imposing laws.

The Blind Man

Paris

Look, where he goes he interrupts the town
—which is not where his darkness is—
like a dark crack going through a clear
light-coloured cup. And the reflection

of things is painted on him as on paper;
he does not take it in.
Only his feeling stirs as if it caught
the world in little waves:

a silence, a resistance; waiting,
he seems to choose somebody, lifts his hand
devotedly and almost festive
as though to give himself in marriage.

Late Autumn in Venice

No longer does the city drift like bait
that catches all emerging days.
The glassy palaces ring out more brittle
against your gaze. The summer hangs

from gardens, like a heap of puppets,
head foremost, wilted, done to death.
But from the forest skeletons, deep down,
determination rises: overnight

the General of the Seas would have to double
the galleys in the wakeful Arsenal,
to tar the morning air with all his fleet

which throngs with threshing oars, and on a sudden,
all flags unfurled to greet the day, seeps on
before a great wind, radiant, charged with fate.

The Ball

You round one, in your flight you give away,
above, the warmth out of two hands,
carefree as if it were your own; what cannot
remain in things—too weightless for them,

too little thing and yet still thing enough
not to glide into us all of a sudden,
invisibly, from all that stands outside
in rigid order—: glided into you

who have not yet decided between fall and flight;
and you abduct the throw and set it free
in your own rise, as if you raised it too;
you stop in curving downwards and you show, above,
the players on a sudden a new spot,
arranging them as for the figure of a dance,

and then, expected, wished-for by them all,
swift, simple, artless, and entirely Nature,
you fall to meet the cup of lifted hands.

The Child

Involuntarily, a long while, they continue
to watch him playing; now and then there turns
his face, round, living, from its profile
and has the clarity and fullness of an hour

that starts and goes on striking to the end.
But dulled with hardship, sluggish from their lives,
the others fail to count the strokes;
and neither do they notice how he bears,

how he bears everything, then too, and still
when, tired, he sits there in his little dress
beside them as if in a waiting-room
and wants to wait for his own time to come.

The Dog

Up there, the image of a world is ever
renewed by glances, and is valid. Only
at times, in secret, something comes and stands
beside him as he pushes through that image

from down below, and different, as he *is*;
and not cast out, and not included either,
as though in doubt, bestowing his own realness
upon the image he forgets, he still

keeps lifting up his face to penetrate it,
in supplication almost, on the verge
of comprehension, close to understanding,
and yet renounces: for he would not *be*.

The Duino Elegies (1912–1922)

The First Elegy

Who, if I cried out, would hear me among the orders
of angels? and even if one of them took me
suddenly to his heart: I should fade in his stronger
existence. For beauty is nothing but the beginning
of terror which we can scarcely bear,
and we marvel at it because it calmly disdains
to destroy us. Every angel is terrible.
And so I contain myself and suppress the call-note of dark
sobbing. Ah, whom are we able to turn to? Not angels,
not men, and the knowing animals sense it already
that we are not very securely
at home in the interpreted world. Perhaps there remains
some tree on a hillside, that we may daily
see it again; there remains for us yesterday's street
and the pampered fidelity of a habit that liked
being with us and therefore remained and did not go.
O and the night, the night when the wind full of cosmic space
feeds on our faces—, longed-for, gently disappointing,
for whom would it not remain, its hardship imminent
for the single heart. The night, is it easier for lovers?
Ah, with each other they merely conceal their fate.
Do you still not know? Fling emptiness out of your arms
into the spaces we breathe; it may be that birds
will feel the expanded air in happier flight.

Yes, the spring-seasons needed you. Some
stars expected you to perceive them.
A wave came surging up from the past,
or a violin gave itself as you were passing
an open window. It all imposed obligation.
But were you equal to it? Did not expectancy always
preoccupy you as if all things announced
to you a beloved one? (Where will you harbour her,
those great strange thoughts going in and out
and often staying with you in the night.)
But sing the lovers when you experience longing,
the fame of their feeling is far from immortal enough;
those—you envy them almost—who were forsaken, and yet

so much more loving than those whose love was requited.
Ever anew start the praise you can never fully accomplish;
think: the hero lives on, and even his end
is to him only a pretext for *being*: his ultimate
birth. But exhausted Nature takes lovers back
into herself as if twice there would not be strength
for such an achievement. Have you enough called to mind
Gaspara Stampa, so that her intenser example of love
may make a girl, whose lover withdrew from her, feel:
'if only I were to become like her'?
Should not these oldest sufferings grow more fruitful
at last? And is it not time that we, loving,
break free from the loved one and, trembling, endure it
thus as the arrow endures the bow-string, gathered
in the leap to be *more* than itself? Staying is nowhere.

Voices, voices. Hear, my heart,
as only the saints have heard: the gigantic call
raised them off the ground; but they, impossible,
continued kneeling and gave it no heed: they heard
so intently. You would not ever be able to bear
the voice of God. But, hear, then, the breathing wind,
the uninterrupted message shaping from silence.
Its rushing sound now reaches you from the young dead.
Whenever you entered, did not their fate
calmly address you in churches at Naples and Rome?
Or the solemn dignity of an inscription absorbed
your attention, as lately the tablet in Santa Maria Formosa.
What do they want of me? gently, to cast aside
the appearance of wrong which now and again
slightly impedes their spirits' pure movement.

True, it is strange to dwell on the earth no longer,
no longer to practise customs scarcely acquired,
not to give the meaning of human future
to roses and other things of particular promise;
to be no longer what one had been
in infinitely anxious hands, and even
to drop one's own name like a broken toy.
Strange, not to continue wishing one's wishes.

Strange to see all, which had once applied, so loosely
fluttering in space. To be dead is hard, full of effort
to catch up on knowledge, until one slowly begins
to grasp some trace of eternity.—But the living
make the mistake of drawing too rigid distinctions.
Angels often (so it is said) do not know
whether they move among living or dead. The eternal
current always rushes all ages through both
realms and, in both, drowns their sound with its own.

They finally need us no longer, those early dead,
one is softly weaned from this earth, as one gently outgrows
the breasts of one's mother. We, though, needing such great
secrets, we, to whom out of grief so often
blissful progress springs forth—: *could* we exist without *them*?
Is the legend in vain that once, in lament for Linos,
daring first music broke barren numbness,
that only in terrified space, which a youth who was almost a god
suddenly left for ever, emptiness swung into that
vibration which charms and consoles and helps us now.

The Second Elegy

Every angel is terrible. Yet, woe is me,
I sing of you, almost-deadly birds of the soul,
apprehending you. Where are the days of Tobias when one of
the most radiant stood at the simple street-door,
for the journey a little disguised, and already no longer terrible;
(a youth to the youth, who looked out with curiosity).
If now from behind the stars the dangerous archangel stepped
only one step downwards and hither: high-up beating,
our own heart would slay us. Who are you?

Early happily-chanced successes, Creation's favourites,
mountain-ranges, dawn-purple ridges
of all that has been created,—the blossoming deity's pollen,
hinges of light, passages, staircases, thrones,
spaces of being, shields of bliss, tumults
of violently rapturous feeling, and suddenly, single,
mirrors drawing up into their faces again
their own beauty that had been streaming away.

For we, when we feel, lose substance; ah we
breathe ourselves out and away; from ember to ember
we emit a fainter scent. Maybe somebody tells us:
yes, you enter into my blood; this room,
spring, is filling with you ... What does it avail,
he cannot hold us, within and around him we fade away.
And those who are beautiful, O who retains them? Appearance
incessantly rises and goes in their faces. Like dew
from the morning grass, like heat from a steaming dish, there rises
from us what is ours. Whither, O smile? O upward glance:
new, warm, vanishing wave of the heart—:
woe is me, yet we *are* it. But does
cosmic space, which we dissolve into, taste of us? Do the angels
only absorb what is theirs, what has streamed
from them—or is in it, sometimes, as if by mistake,
some of our being as well? Are we mingled into their features
only so much as that vagueness is mingled into the faces
of pregnant women? They do not perceive within the whirl
of their return to themselves. (How should they perceive it).

If they understood it, lovers might strangely
converse in the night-air. For it appears that we
are kept secret by everything. See, the trees *are*;
the houses in which we dwell, still exist. Only we,
like air interchanged, move past everything.
And all combines to pass us over in silence, partly perhaps
as shame, and partly as an ineffable hope.

Lovers, you who suffice in each other, you
I ask about us. You grasp each other. Do you have proofs?
See, it happens to me that my hands grow conscious
of each other or that my worn face finds
forbearance in them. That gives me a little feeling.
Yet who could, for that, already dare to *exist*?
But you who grow in the other's rapture
until, overwhelmed, he implores you: not *more*—;
you who under each other's hands
grow more copious like years of abundant vintage;
you who at times fade away only because the other
completely prevails: you I ask about us. I know
that you so blissfully touch each other because the caress
lasts, because the place which you, tender ones, cover
does not vanish; because you feel pure duration beneath it.
Thus, from embrace, you almost expect eternity.
Yet when you have overcome the terrors of first
glances, the longing at the window, the first
walk together, *once*, through the garden:
lovers, are you *not then*, still the same? When you raise
each other to your lips and commence—: drink unto drink:
O how the drinker then strangely withdraws from the action.

Did not the caution of human gesture on Attic stelae
surprise you? were love and farewell not placed so lightly
on shoulders as if they were wrought of a substance other
than we use? Remember the hands, how they rest without pressure
although there stands strength in the torsos. By that
they knew, those who mastered themselves: so far it is us,
thus to touch one another is ours; the gods
urge us more forcibly onwards. But that is concern of the gods.

Would that we, too, found some pure and mitigated and slender
humanity, one, our own, strip of fertile ground
between stream and rock. For our heart still transcends us
as theirs did. And we can no longer gaze after it
into images soothing it, nor into god-like
bodies in which it assumes a superior restraint.

The Third Elegy

One thing, to sing the loved one: another, alas,
to sing the hidden, guilty river-god of the blood.
He whom she knows from afar, her young lover, what does he
know of that lord of desires who in him, in his loneliness, often,
before she had soothed him, and often as though she did not exist,
raised his god-head, dripping, ah, from inscrutable depths,
and roused the night to an infinite uproar.
O the Neptune of the blood, O his terrible trident.
O the dark wind of his chest from the twisted conch-shell.
Hear how the night curves away and grows hollow.
Stars, are not *you* the source of the lover's delight
in the face of his loved one? Has not his intimate insight
into her pure face come from the pure constellations?

Not you, alas, it was not his mother
who tautened his brows into such an expectant arch.
Not with you, young girl, so tenderly conscious of him, not with you
did his lips begin to curve into richer expression.
Do you suppose that in lightly approaching
you could have shaken him so, you who wander like morning wind?
Yes, you frightened his heart; but older terrors
swept into him in that moment of impact.
Call him ... you cannot call him entirely away from dark involvement.
Indeed, he *wants* to, he does break free; relieved, he settles
into your sheltering heart, and takes and begins himself there.
But did he begin himself, ever?
Mother, *you* made him small, it was you who began him;
to you he was new, and over those new eyes you bent
the friendly world and warded off the one that was alien.
Where, ah, where are the years when your slender form
stood artlessly in the way of the surging chaos?
There was much you hid from him then; the nightly mistrusted
room was made harmless by you, and out of your heart full of refuge
you mingled more human space with the space of his night.
Not in the darkness, no, in your nearer presence
you placed the night-light; it shone as though out of friendship.
Nowhere a creaking you did not explain with a smile
as if you had long known *when* the floor would act in that way ...

And he listened to you, and was soothed. It could do so much,
your gentle rising; tall, cloaked, his Fate
stepped behind the wardrobe, and his easily shifting
restless future merged into fold of the curtain.

And he, as he lay there, relieved, under sleepy
eyelids dissolving your light form's sweetness
into the foretaste of sleep, *appeared*
protected ... *Within* him, though: who could stem,
ward off, within him the floods of origin?
Ah, there was no caution in him who was sleeping; asleep,
but dreaming, but feverish: what he engaged in!
New and shy, how entangled he was,
with ever-extending tendrils of inner event
interlaced to patterns already, to strangling growth, to forms
chasing like beasts. How he gave himself.—Loved.
Loved his innermost being, its wilderness, this
primeval forest within him on whose silent downfall
his heart stood, light-green. Loved. Left it, and went
from his own roots down into mighty beginnings
where his little birth was already outlived. Loving,
descended into the older blood, the ravines
where horror lay, satiated still with his fathers. And every
terror knew him, winked, and appeared informed.
Yes, frightfulness smiled ... You have seldom
smiled so tenderly, mother. How should he not love it
since it was smiling at him? Before he loved *you*
he had loved it: when you were bearing him it was there,
dissolved in the water that lightens the budding child.

We do not love the same way as flowers,
out of one single year; immemorial sap
rises into our arms when we love. O maiden,
this: we loved *within* us, not one, one to come,
but numberless teeming; not one single child,
but the fathers who rest like shattered mountains
within our depth; but the dried-up river bed
of former mothers—; but the entire
soundless landscape under clouded or clear
impending destiny—: *this* preceded you, maiden.

And you, what are you able to know—, you evoked
ages long past in your lover. What feelings
burrowed upwards from beings long gone. What women
hated you there. What sinister men
you roused in the veins of the youth. Dead children
wanted to reach you ... Gently, O gently,
show him a tenderly done reassuring day's-work,
lead him close to the garden, give him the nights'
counterbalance ...
                    Compose him ...

The Fourth Elegy

O tree of life, when are you wintry?
We are discordant. We are not informed
like birds of passage. Suddenly,
outrun and late, we force ourselves on winds
and we come down on an impassive pond.
Bloom and decay are simultaneously our knowledge.
And somewhere there roam lions still, and while
they are magnificent, they know no impotence.

But we, when we are wholly concentrated on the one,
already feel the opposition of the other.
Our first response is enmity. Do lovers
—who had expected spaces, hunt, and home—
not always step up to brinks, one in the other.
There is a ground of contrast, for a moment's sketch,
laboriously prepared, that we might see it;
for there is great exactness for our sake.
We do not know the contours of emotion,
we only know what shapes them from outside.
Who has not sat in fear before the curtain
of his own heart? It rose: the scenery was Parting.
Easy to understand. The well-known garden,
softly swaying: only then the dancer came.
Not *he*. Enough. However light he feigns to be,
he is disguised and he becomes a bourgeois
and, through his kitchen, walks into his flat.
I will not have these half-filled masks,
rather the doll. It is full. I will
endure its body and the wire and the face
of appearance. Here. I face it. And even
if the lights go out, and even if I am told:
Nothing more—, and even if from the stage
emptiness drifts with the grey draught of air,
and even if none of my silent ancestors
sits with me any longer, no woman, not even
that boy any more, with his brown squinting eye:
Yet I stay on. For there is always watching.
Is it not so? You whose life tasted bitter
because of me—you, father, tasting mine;

ever again, as I was growing up, you tasted
the turbid first infusion of my inner
compulsion; occupied with such an unknown future's
after-taste, you searched my clouded upward glance
you who, my father, since you died, are often
afraid within my inward hope, and who abandon
the equanimity the dead have, realms
of equanimity, for my small share of fate,
is it not so? And you, is it not so,
you who have loved me for the small beginning
of love for you, from which I always turned away
because the space within your faces changed,
while I was loving it, to cosmic space
in which you were no longer ... If I feel I want
to wait before the puppet-stage, no, so intently
to gaze there at it that finally, to counterbalance
my gaze, an angel has to step there as an actor
and jerk the puppets upwards—
angel and doll: then at last there is performance.
Then there unites what we incessantly disrupt
by our existence. Only then there forms
out of our seasons, the whole movement's cycle
and, over and above us all, the angel acts.
Those who are dying, should they not surmise
how much pretence there is in all
that we accomplish here. It all is not
what it purports to be. O hours in childhood
when there was more behind the figures
than merely what had passed, and not the future
before us. We were growing, though, and sometimes urgent
in wanting soon to be grown-up—for their sake, partly,
who had no longer anything except their being
grown-up. Yet, in our separateness, we rejoiced in
what lasted, and we stood there in the intermediate
space between the world and toy,
upon a spot that from the earliest beginning
had been intended for a pure event.

Who shows a child as it stands there? Who places
it in a constellation, puts the measure
of distance in its hand? Who makes its death

from grey bread that turns hard,—or leaves it
within the round mouth, like the core
of some fair apple? ... Murderers are
easy to comprehend. But: death
the whole of death, already before life
so gently to contain and not be bad—
is indescribable.

The Fifth Elegy

But who, tell me, *are* they, these acrobats, slightly more fleeting
even than we are, from early days
urgently wrong—for whose, whose sake—
by a never satisfied will? But it wrings them,
bends them, slings them and swings them,
hurls them and catches them back; as if out of oiled,
more slippery, air they come down
onto the threadbare carpet thinned
by their eternal leap, this lost
carpet there in the universe.
Laid on like a plaster as if the suburb
sky had hurt the earth.
                              Hardly there,
erect, there, and shown: the capital letter
of Standing ... already, the strongest
men are rolled over again, for a jest, by the ever
coming grip, as by August the Strong at table
a pewter plate.

Ah and around this
centre the rose of onlooking:
blooms and unblossoms. Around this
pounder, the pistil, met by its own
blossoming pollen, fecundated again for the sham-fruit
of reluctance never conscious,—glittering
with thinnest surface of lightly sham-smiling reluctance.

There, the withered, the wrinkled lifter,
the old one who now merely drums,
contracted in his enormous skin as though it had once
contained *two* men, and the one were already
lying in the churchyard, and he had survived him,
deaf, and sometimes a little
confused, in his widowed skin.

But the young one, the man, as if the son of a nape
and a nun: tautly and firmly filled
with muscles and simpleness.

Oh you
whom a suffering once, when still small,
received as toys in one of its long
convalescences ...

You that fall, unripe,
with the thud only fruits know,
daily a hundred times off the tree of mutually built-up
movement, (the tree that, more swiftly than water,
has spring and summer and autumn within a few minutes)—
fall off and rebound on the grave:
sometimes, in half a pause, your face
wants to begin conveying affection across to your mother
who seldom was tender; but it gets lost—this timidly,
scarcely attempted face—on your body
that spends it on surface ... Again
the man claps his hands for the leap, and before
pain can become more distinct
close to your ever galloping heart, the burning
in the soles of your feet comes before it, its origin,
with a few physical tears chased hurriedly into your eyes.
And yet, blindly,
the smile ...

Angel! O take it, pluck it, the small-flowered plant of healing.
Shape a vase for it, store it! Place it among
those joys not yet open to us; in a lovely urn
praise it with flowery, sweeping inscription: '*Subrisio saltat*'.
Then you, lovely one,
you who are mutely passed over
by the most exquisite joys.
Perhaps your frills are happy for you—,
or, over your young full breasts,
the green metallic
silk feels endlessly pampered, lacks nothing.
You,
market-fruit of equanimity,
ever differently placed upon all swaying scales of balance,
publicly, there, among shoulders.
Where, o where is that place—I carry it in my heart—
where they still were far from mastering it, still
falling off each other like mounting, not quite

pairing animals;—
where weights are still heavy;
where, from their rods that are twirling in vain,
the plates still
reel ...
And, suddenly, there, in this toilsome Nowhere, suddenly
the ineffable spot where the pure Too Little
incomprehensibly changes—, switches around
into that empty Too Much.
Where the many-digited total
resolves itself into zero.

Squares, O square in Paris, infinite show-place,
where Madame Lamotte, the modiste,
winds and twists the restless roads of the earth,
endless ribbons, and from them devises new bows,
frills, flowers, cockades, artificial fruits
—all in unnatural colours—to match the cheap
winter hats of Fate.
....

Angel: supposing there were a place that we do not know,
and there, on an ineffable carpet, lovers—who here
never attain ability—showed their bold
soaring figures of heart-flight,
their towers of desire, their ladders
long since, where ground never was,
leaning only against each other, trembling—and were *able* to do it
before the surrounding spectators, the noiseless uncountable dead:
Would these then throw their last, their ever saved-up,
ever concealed, and unknown to us, their eternally
valid coins of happiness down before the at last
genuinely smiling pair on the soothed
carpet?

The Sixth Elegy

Fig-tree, for me it has so long been full of meaning
how you almost entirely neglect to flower
and drive, un-extolled, your pure secret
into timely resolute fruit.
Like the tube of a fountain, your twisted twigs
thrust upwards your sap, and up: and it leaps out of sleep,
almost not wakening, into the bliss of its sweetest achievement.
See: like into the swan the god

                    … But we linger,
alas, it becomes us to flower; we enter,
betrayed, the belated core of our ultimate fruit.
In a few the pressure of action mounts with such force—
they already stand up and they glow in the fullness of heart
when temptation to flower, like softened night air,
touches the youth of their mouths and their eye-lids:
heroes, perhaps, and those who are destined to pass beyond early,
whose veins have been differently twisted by gardening Death.
These rush onwards: ahead of their own
smile, like the team of horses in mild
moulded reliefs at Karnak ahead of the conquering king.

The hero indeed is strangely akin to the youthfully dead.
Permanence does not concern him. His rise is existence; continuously,
he withdraws himself and enters the changed constellation
of his constant danger. There only few could find him. But Fate
—sombre in passing us over in silence—
all of a sudden enraptured,
sings him into the storm of her up-surging world.
Not one do I hear as I hear him. His darkened tone
suddenly passes through me with the streaming air.

How then I should like to hide from longing: O would that I were,
would that I were a boy and were granted to come to it yet
and were sitting propped upon arms yet to be and were reading of Samson,
how his mother had first given birth to nothing and, later, to all.

Was he not hero already within you, O mother, and did not
there his imperious choice already begin, within you?
Thousands were brewing in the womb and wanting to be him,
but see: he seized and excluded, chose and was able.
And when he shattered columns it was when he broke
out of the world of your body and into the narrower world
where he still continued to choose and be able. O mothers of heroes,
O sources of ravaging streams! You, ravines into which,
high-up from the brink of the heart, lamenting,
maidens had already hurled themselves, victims-to-be for the son.
For the hero rushed onwards through resting-places of love,
each single heart-beat that meant him raised him beyond it,
turning away already, he stood at the end of all smiles, different.

The Seventh Elegy

Wooing no longer, not wooing, voice that outgrew it,
shall be the note of your cry; though you cried as pure as the bird
when the rising season uplifts him, almost forgetting
he is a sorrowful creature and not merely one single heart
which she flings to brightness, to intimate skies. Like him
you would woo, no less—to make her grow conscious of you,
invisible yet, your silent companion in whom a reply
gradually wakes and increases in warmth while she listens—
the fellow-feeling, aglow, for your own emboldened feeling.
O and spring would understand—, there is not a spot
that does not give voice to the note of annunciation. At first
that little, questioning pipe which a pure, an affirming day
in silence widely surrounds with magnifying stillness.
Then ascending the steps, ascending the call-steps up to the dreamt-of
temple of the future—; the trill then, the fountain
apprehending already the downward fall for the thrusting jet
in a promiseful play … And summer before it.
Not only all the mornings of summer—, not only
the way they change into day and shine with beginning.
Not only the days which are gentle round flowers and which,
above, are strong and powerful round the configured trees.
Not only the devotion of these unfolded forces,
not only the paths, not only the evening meadows,
not only, after late thunder, the breathing clarity,
not only approaching sleep and a vague surmise in the evening …
but the nights! But the lofty, the summer
nights, but the stars, the stars of the earth.
O to be dead once and have an infinite knowledge
of all of the stars: for how, how, how to forget them!

See, then I called the lover. But not only *she*
would come … There would come, from weak graves,
maidens, and stand there … For how can I limit,
how, the call that is called? Those who sank below
are still seeking earth.—You children, a thing
that has once been grasped here would be valid for many.
Do not think that Fate is more than what childhood was densely full of;
how often you outdistanced the loved one, panting,
panting after a blissful run, towards nothing, out into the open.

To be here is wonderful. You, maidens, knew it, you too
who, as it seemed, went without, sank under—, you, in the vilest
streets of the cities, festering, or open for refuse.
Because an hour was granted to each one, perhaps
not quite an hour, a span that could scarcely be measured
by measures of time, in between two whiles, when she had
an existence. Everything. Veins full of existence.
But it happens so easily that we forget what our laughing neighbour
does not confirm or envy us for. We want visibly
to hold it upwards, whereas the most visible bliss
reveals itself to us only when we transform it within.

Nowhere, beloved, will there be world but within. Our life
passes in transformation. And, ever diminishing,
there vanishes what is outside. Where there once had been
a lasting house, a thought-out construction slashes itself across it,
entirely belonging to thought as though it still stood in the brain.
The spirit of the time creates for himself capacious garners of power
as shapeless as is the straining urge which he gains from all things.
Temples he knows no longer. These, the lavish gifts of the heart,
we save up more secretly. Yes, where there still is a thing
that outlasts, a thing once prayed, served, knelt—, it already
holds itself out, as it is, into the Invisible.
Many perceive it no more, but without the advantage
of building it now *within*, with pillars and statues, *greater*!

Every dull turn of the world has such who are thus disinherited,
whose is not what has been and not yet what comes next.
For even the next is remote for man. This shall not bewilder us;
it shall strengthen in us our retaining the form
we still recognise. Once this *stood* among men,
it stood in the midst of destructive fate, in the midst
of not-knowing-whither it stood as though it existed, and bent
stars towards itself from secured heavens.
Angel, to you I will show it yet, *there*! in your gaze
it shall stand at last saved, now finally upright.
Columns, pylons, the Sphinx, the striving thrust,
grey, from a fading or foreign town, of the dome.

Was it not a miracle? Angel, O gaze in wonder for *we* are it,
we, O you great one, tell them that we have achieved this, my breath
is not sufficient for giving praise. Thus we have, nonetheless,
not neglected using the spaces, these generous spaces,
these, *our* spaces. (How frightfully large they must be
since thousands of years of our feeling do not overfill them).
But a tower was great, was it not? O Angel, it was—,
great, beside even you? Chartres was great—and music
reached up higher still and transcended us. But
even only a woman who loves, oh, alone in the night at her window …
did she not reach to your knees?
                    Do not think I am wooing,
Angel, and even if I were wooing you! You do not come.
For my call-of-appeal is always full of Away;
against such a powerful current you cannot stride.
My call is like an extended arm. And its hand,
open above for grasping, remains
open before you like warding off and like warning,
Inapprehensible one, high up there.

The Eighth Elegy

to Rudolf Kassner

The eyes of all the living creatures see the open
But *our* eyes are as though reversed
and set around them like encircling traps,
round their free path that leads them outwards.
Our knowledge of what *is* outside
comes to us from the animal's gaze alone,
for we already turn the young child round and force it
backwards to see formation—not the open,
so deep within the animal's face. Free from death.
Death we alone see; the free animal
has always its eclipse behind it
and God in front, and when it moves
it moves into eternity, like fountains flowing.
We never have, not for a single day,
pure space before us, into which the flowers
infinitely open. It is always World
and never Nowhere without Not:
the element unsupervised and pure, one breathes
and infinitely knows and does not covet.
Quietly, a child may lose himself to it,
and then is jerked away. Or someone dies and *is* it.
For close to death one does not see death any more
and stares *beyond*, perhaps as with the animal's wide gaze.
Lovers, if there were not the other who obstructs
the view, draw close to it, and marvel …
As if through oversight, behind the other
it is revealed to them … But neither can
get past the other, and world returns to them once more.
Always turned towards Creation, all we see
is only a reflection of the open,
darkened by ourselves. Or that a silent animal
raises his gaze which calmly passes through us.
This is what fate means: being opposite,
nothing but that, and always opposite.
If consciousness such as is ours, existed

in the sure animal which on a different course
is coming towards us, he would force us round
with his own movement. But his being
is infinite to him, un-grasped, and with no insight
into his state, pure, like his outward gaze.
Where we see Future he sees Everything,
in Everything himself, for ever whole.

Yet, in the watchfully warm animal
there is the sorrow and the weight of a great sadness.
To him as well, there always clings
what often overwhelms us—a remembrance
as though what we are striving for, had been
already closer, truer, infinitely tender
in its attachment. Here, all is distance,
and there it had been breath. The second home,
after that first one, seems ambiguous and unstable.
O bliss of *little* creatures that *remain*
forever in the womb that brought them forth;
the happiness, o, of the gnat which even when it weds
still leaps *within*: the womb is all.
And see the half-assurance of the bird
which almost, through its origin, knows both,
as if it were the soul of an Etruscan,
of a dead man who rests within a space
but whose recumbent figure on it forms a lid.
And how perplexed a creature is that has to fly,
and issued from a womb. As though it took
fright of itself, it zigzags through the air,
as a crack goes through a cup. The bat's track thus
rends through the porcelain of the evening.

And we: onlookers, always, everywhere,

turned towards it all, and never towards the open!
It overcrowds us. We arrange it, and it loses substance.
We re-arrange it and ourselves lose substance then.

Who has thus turned us round that we,
whatever we may do, are in the attitude
of one who goes away? As he,
on the last hill which once more shows him
all his valley, turns and stops and lingers—
we live, for ever taking leave.

The Ninth Elegy

Why, when this set time of life may be spent
as laurel, a little darker than all other green,
with little waves, on the border of every leaf
(like the smile of a wind)—: why then have
to do what is human—, and, shunning fate
to be longing for fate? ...

                           Oh, not because happiness *is*,
this precipitate profit of imminent loss.
Not from curiosity, not to practice the heart
that would be in the laurel, too ...
But because being here is much, and because
all that is here, and is transient, apparently needs us
and strangely concerns us. Us, the most transient of all.
Everything *once*, only *once*. *Once*, and no more.
And we also *once*. And never again. But having been this
once, although only *once*: having been
of *this earth*, appears irrevocable.

And thus we press forward and want to accomplish it,
want to contain it within our simple hands, in the gaze
filled more to an overflow, and in the speechless heart.
Want to become it. Give it to whom? Would most of all like
keeping it all for ever ... Ah, into that other relation, alas,
what is there one takes across? Not Seeing,
slowly learnt here, and no event of the Here. None.
Sufferings, then. Then, above all, the hardship of life,
the long experience of love, then—that is,
everything that is un-sayable. But
later, what does it avail among stars: they are *better* un-sayable.
The wanderer, too, does not bring from the slope of the hill
a handful of earth, to us all un-sayable, down to the valley,
but a word he has won, a pure word, the yellow and blue
gentian. Are we, perhaps, *here* in order to say:
House, Bridge, Well, Gate, Jug, Fruit-tree, Window,—
at most: Column, Tower ... but to *say*, do you grasp it,
oh to say them *thus* as things themselves had never
so ardently known to exist. Is it not the secret cunning of this
secretive earth, when it urges lovers onwards, to make
all things and everything rapturous in their emotion?

Threshold: how much for two
lovers to wear out a little their own, the older,
threshold, they too, after many before
and before those to come ... lightly.

Here is the time of the Sayable, *here* is its home.
Speak and confess. More than ever before,
things that can be experienced are falling away
for what, supplanting them, takes their place, is deed without image.
Deed under crusts that readily split when the action within
outgrows and adopts other outlines.
Between the hammers, our heart
lives on, as, between the teeth, the tongue which nevertheless,
which yet continues to praise.

Praise the world to the Angel, not the un-sayable world, to him
you cannot boast with the splendour you felt; in the universe
where he feels with more feeling, you are a beginner. And therefore
show him a thing that is simple and, moulded by one generation
after the other, lives as our own, in our gaze and next to our hand.
Say the things to him. And he will stand in profounder wonder:
as you stood beside the roper in Rome or the potter in Egypt.
Show him how happy a thing can be, how guiltless and ours,
how even lamenting grief purely decides on adopting form,
serves as a thing, or dies into a thing—, and, beyond,
it escapes, full of bliss, from the violin. These
things that live in passing away understand that you praise them.
Transient, they rely for salvation on us, the most transient of all.
Want us to change them entirely within our invisible hearts
into—O endlessly—into ourselves! no matter whoever we are.

Earth, is it not this that you want: invisibly
to arise within us?—Is it not your dream,
sometimes to be invisible?—Earth! Invisible!
What is your urgent command, if not transformation?
Earth, you dear one, I will. Oh believe me,
your springs are no longer required to win me for you,
one, ah one single spring, is already too much for my blood.
Since early beginning I have been ineffably yours.
You always were right, and your sacred
inspiration is: friendly death.

See, I live. Out of what? Neither childhood nor future
diminishes ... Superabundant existence
wells up in my heart.

The Tenth Elegy

May I, when at the end of this cruel insight,
sing jubilation and praise to assenting angels.
May not one of the firm-hammered keys of my heart
fail to evoke response by touching on slack, uncertain
or bursting strings. May my streaming face
lend me more radiance; may inconspicuous weeping
blossom. O nights of grief, how dear you will be to me then.
Why did I not receive you, inconsolable sisters,
more submissively kneeling, did not surrender myself more freely
into your free-flowing hair? We, the wasters of sorrows.
How we gaze ahead of them, out into sad permanence,
to see if perhaps they might come to an end. But they are
our foliage lasting through winter, our dark evergreen,
one of the inner year's seasons—not only
season—are place, and settlement, camp, soil and dwelling.

Strange, alas, are the streets of the City of Suffering
where, in the sham silence of sound drowned by sound,
there swaggers, the cast poured forth from the mould of emptiness,
blatant, the gilded noise, the monument bursting apart.
O how an angel would tread underfoot without trace their market
   of consolation
adjoined by the church which they bought ready-made:
clean, disillusioned and closed as a post-office is on a Sunday.
But outside there is always a ripple along the fringe of the fair.
Swings of freedom! Divers and jugglers of zeal!
And the shooting-range figures of prettified happiness,
targets jerking and tinnily clinking whenever
hit by some better marksman. From cheers to chance
he goes staggering on, as booths serving every kind of curiosity
solicit attention, bawl, and beat drums. But there is, in particular,
for adults, the breeding of money on view, anatomical,
not for amusement only: the sex part of money,
the whole of it, all the act—instructive, ensuring
fertility...
       Oh, but quite close, just beyond it,
behind the last hoarding plastered with posters for 'Deathless',
the bitter beer that seems sweet to those who consume it

when, as they drink, they continually chew fresh distractions,
just at the back of the hoarding, there, just behind, it is *real*:
children at play, and lovers holding each other, aside,
gravely, in shabby grass, and dogs obeying their instincts.
The youth is drawn farther away; it may be that he loves
a youthful Lament … Behind her, he walks into meadows. She says:
'Far away. We are living out there …'

                    Where? And he follows.
He is touched by her bearing. Her shoulder, her neck—perhaps
she is of noble descent. But he leaves her, turns back,
faces round, and waves … What does it avail? She is a Lament.

Only the youthful dead, in their first condition
of timeless serenity, of becoming weaned,
follow her lovingly. Girls
she waits for, befriends them. Shows them gently
what she wears on her person. The pearls of suffering,
the finely woven veils of endurance.—Youths
she walks with in silence.

But, where they live, in the valley, one of the older
Laments responds to the youth when he asks. 'We were once',
she says, 'a great family, we, the Laments. Our fathers
worked the mines in those towering mountains; at times,
    among humans,
you find a piece of polished primeval suffering
or, from an ancient volcano, drossy petrified wrath.
Yes, that had its origin there. We were rich once'.

And leading him lightly through the spacious landscape of Laments,
she shows him the columns of temples, the ruins
of strongholds from which, in the past, the sovereign princes
of the House of Lament had wisely governed the land.
Shows him the tall tear-trees, the fields of flowering sadness
(known to the living only as tender foliage);
shows him the grazing creatures of grief—and at times
a startled bird, in its level flight through their lifted gaze,
traces the long-drawn trail of its lonely cry.
In the evening she leads him up to the graves of the eldest
of the House of Lament, the sibyls and seers.
But, night drawing near, they move more softly, and soon,

moon-like, there rises before them, guarding all things,
the sepulchral monument. Brother to that by the Nile,
the lofty Sphinx—the reticent chamber's face.
And they marvel at the regal head which, for ever,
has silently poised human vision
upon the scale of the stars.

His glance does not grasp it, dizzy
with early death. But her gaze
starts an owl from behind the rim of the *pshent*.
Brushing in slowly descending flight
along the cheek with the richest curve,
it softly traces across the new
death-given hearing, over an open
double page, the indescribable outline.

And, higher, the stars. New ones. Stars of the land of suffering.
The Lament slowly names them: 'There,
see: the Horseman, the Staff and they call the more crowded
constellation the Garland of Fruit. Then, nearer the Pole:
Cradle, Way, The Burning Book, Doll, and Window.
But in the southern sky, pure as in the palm
of a blessed hand, the translucid M
which signifies Mothers ...'

But he, the dead youth, must go on, and the older Lament
silently takes him as far as the gorge
where it gleams in the moonlight:
the Source of Joy. With reverence
she names it, and says: 'Among humans,
it is a carrying stream.'

They stand at the foot of the mountains.
And there she embraces him, weeping.

Alone, he climbs to the Hills of Primeval Suffering.
And in soundless fate not even his steps make a sound.

But if they, the endlessly dead, evoked a symbol to us,
look, they might point to the catkins hanging from bare
hazels, or else bring to mind
the rain that falls on dark earth in the spring.

And we, who think of *ascending*
happiness, would experience
the feeling which almost startles
when what is happy *falls*.

from *Sonnets to Orpheus (1922)*

ONE

I

A tree ascended there. O pure transcension!
O Orpheus sings! O tall tree in the ear!
And all was mute. Yet even in that utter muteness
a new beginning, beckoning and change arose.

Creatures of silence thronged out of the clear
untangled wood from lair and nest;
and it appeared that not from cunning
they were so still within themselves, nor fear,

but hearing. Bellow, roar and scream
seemed little in their hearts. And where before
there barely was a hut that might receive it,

a hiding-place of darkest longing,
its entrance flanked by quivering posts—
there you created temples in their sense of hearing.

II

A maiden almost, she emerged
from this concordant bliss of song and lyre,
and sparkled through her vernal veils,
and made herself a bed within my ear.

And slept in me. Her sleep was everything:
the trees I ever marvelled at, and distance
that can be felt, the meadow grasped in feeling,
and every wondering about myself.

She slept the world. How have you, singing god,
perfected her that she did not desire
to be awake? See, she took shape and slept.

Where is her death? Oh will you introduce
This theme before your song is spent?—
Where is she sinking from me? ... Almost a maiden ...

III

A god can do it. But how is a man
to follow after, through the narrow lyre?
His mind is discord. Where two heartways intersect
there stands no temple for Apollo.

Song, thus as taught by you, is not desire,
not striving after something in the end attained;
song is sheer being. Easy for the god.
But when do we exist? And when does he

expend the earth and stars on our existence?
It is not *this*, youth, not your loving, even
if then this voice will force your mouth wide open—

learn to forget your sudden song. It fades away.
Real singing is a different breath.
A breath as such. A stirring in the god. A breeze.

IV

You who love tenderly, step now and then
into the breath not intended for you,
let it divide as it touches your cheeks,
behind you it quivers, united again.

You who are blessed, you who are whole,
you who seem the beginning of hearts;
bows for arrows and targets for arrows,
your smile everlasting when shining through tears.

Do not fear suffering; heaviness—
give it back to the weight of the earth;
mountains are heavy, heavy the seas.

Even the trees you planted as children
have long grown too heavy for you to sustain.
Ah, but the breezes ... ah, but space ...

V

Set up no stone memorial. Let the rose
for his sake blossom every year.
For it is Orpheus. His metamorphosis
in this one and in this. We need not search

for other names. Where is singing
it once for all is Orpheus. He who comes and goes.
Is it not much already if at times he lingers
a few days longer than the bowl of roses?

O how he has to vanish, so that you may grasp it!
Though he himself may be afraid of vanishing.
And as his word transcends the Here

he is already where you cannot follow.
The lattice of the lyre does not constrain his hands.
And he obeys by stepping out beyond.

VII

Praising, that's it! Appointed to praise,
he came forth like ore from the stone's
silence. His heart, O impermanent winepress
of wine unending to man.

His voice never fails for earthly dust
when he is inspired by divine example.
All becomes vineyard, all becomes cluster
ripened in his responsive South.

Neither the mould of kings in tombs
nor that a shadow falls from the gods
gives the lie to his praise.

One of the messengers ever attending,
he holds vessels with praiseworthy fruits
far through the doors of the dead.

XI

Look at the sky. Is there no constellation
called the 'Horseman'? For this earthy pride
goes strangely deep with us. This, and a second
urging it on, and curbing, borne by it.

Is the sinewy nature of our being
not like this: spurred on, and then reined in?
Path and turning. At a touch, direction.
New horizons. And the two are one.

Are they, though? Or does not either
mean the path they both pursue? Divided
inexpressibly by pasture and by table.

Even stellar union is deceptive.
For a while, though, let us yet take pleasure
in believing in the image. This suffices.

XIV

We share our days with flower, vine-leaf, fruit.
They do not speak the language only of the year.
Out of the dark a multi-coloured revelation rises
and gleams, it may be, with the envy of the dead

who are bestowing strength upon the earth.
What do we know about the part they play in this?
It has long been the custom of the dead
to mix their marrow freely with the clay.

The question, though, is: do they do it gladly?
And do these fruits, the work of heavy slaves,
push upwards, clenched, to us, their masters?

Are *they* the masters, sleeping by the roots
and granting us from their abundance
this hybrid thing of silent strength and kisses?

XVI

You, my friend, are lonely because …
We, with words and with finger-pointing,
gradually make the world our own,
maybe its weakest, most perilous part.

Who would point to a scent with his fingers?—
But of the powers that threaten us
you feel many … You know the dead,
and you take fright at the spell.

Look, together, we now must bear
piecework and parts as if that were the whole.
To help you is hard. Above all: do not plant

me in your heart. I should grow too fast.
But *my* master's hand I will guide, and say:
Here. This is Esau in his rough hide.

XVIII

Lord, do you hear the New
droning and throbbing?
Heralds are coming
this to extol.

There is no hearing whole
in the commotion,
yet the machine-part now
asks to be praised.

See the machine: how it
rolls and takes vengeance,
weakens, distorts us.

Though it draws strength from us,
let it, dispassionate,
serve us, and drive.

XX

But, Master, o what shall I offer you, tell me,
you who have taught the creatures their ear?—
My recollections of a spring day,
its evening, in Russia—a horse …

Alone, the white horse came up from the village,
at a foreleg's fetlock the tethering-block,
to spend the night in the meadows alone;
how the shock of his mane beat against

his neck in the rhythm of high spirits,
his galloping crudely impeded.
How they leapt, the springs of his blood!

He felt the distances, felt them indeed!
he sang and he heard—your cycle of myths
was closed within him.
               I offer: his image.

XXIII

O only *then* when flight
no longer, self-sufficient
and for its own sake alone,
soars into quiet skies

to play, in luminous profiles,
as the accomplished tool,
the darling of winds,
securely wheeling and slim,—

only when a pure 'Whither?'
of growing machines
outweighs boyish pride

will, whelmed with achievement,
he who has neared the distances
be what his lonely flying attains.

XXIV

Shall we disown our age-old friends,
the never wooing great gods, because the hard
steel we have sternly trained does not know them,
or suddenly look for them on a map?

Those powerful friends who take our dead
brush at no point against our wheels.
We have set our banquets, our baths, far aside
and always outdistance their messengers

long since too slow for us. Lonelier now, completely
dependent on each other without knowing each other,
we no longer shape our paths as lovely meanders

but as straight lines. Now the former fires
burn in steam-boilers only and have ever larger
hammers. But we lose our strength like swimmers.

XXV

Once more will I now recall you, you whom I knew
like a flower, without even knowing its name,
and show you to them, you who were taken for ever,
beautiful playmate of the invincible cry.

Dancer who suddenly, all hesitation, paused
as though her youngness were being cast in bronze,
grieving and listening—. Then, from the powers on high,
music descended into her altered heart.

Sickness was near. Overcome by shadows already,
her blood coursed more darkly, yet, as if fleetingly doubted,
swept to its natural springtime once more.

Again and again it gleamed of the Earth, interrupted
by falling and darkness. Until, after terrible throbbing,
it passed through the hopelessly open door.

XXVI

You, the divine one whose song never ceased till the end—
the throng of the slighted maenads falling upon you,
you overlaid their screaming with harmony, beautiful god,
from among the destroyers there rose your creative theme.

No one there could destroy your head or the lyre,
however they wrestled and raved; and the sharp
stones they hurled at your heart became gentle
as soon as they touched you, and gifted with hearing.

Inflamed with vengeance, they finally broke you,
your song still lingering on in lions and rocks,
in trees and in birds. You are singing there still.

O, you lost god! You unending trace!
Because you were torn apart and scattered by hatred
are we the hearers now and a voice of Nature.

TWO

II

As at times the hastily nearer
sheet takes the master's *real* stroke:
thus the mirrors often absorb
the maidens' sacredly only smile

when they are trying the morning, alone,—
or in the gleam of the serving lights.
And into the breathing of real faces,
later, falls nothing but a reflection.

What have eyes once been gazing into
the fire-places' sooty, long fading glow:
gazes of life, for ever lost.

Ah, the Earth's, who knows her losses?
Only he who would, nonetheless giving praise,
sing the heart born into the whole.

IV

This is the creature which has never been.
They did not know that, and in any case
they loved the way it moved, its poise, the neck,
the quiet radiance of its tranquil gaze.

It *was* not. But because they loved it, a pure creature
arose to life. They always left some space.
And in that open space preserved apart
it lightly raised its head, with scarcely any need

to be. They fed it, not with grain, but always with
the possibility it might exist.
And this imbued the creature with such strength

its brow put forth a horn. A single horn.
All white, it came up to a virgin—and it *was*,
there in the silver mirror and in her.

V

Flower-muscle, gradually admitting
the anemone's whole meadow morning
till the loud skies' polyphonic
light pours into its lap—

muscle of an infinite reception,
tautened in the quiet starry blossom,
sometimes overpowered by such fullness
that the sunset's call to rest

scarcely can turn back to you
the rime of petals sprung wide open:
you, resolve and strength of *many* worlds!

We, the violent, continue longer.
But in which of all lives, *when* at last
are we open and receptive?

VI

Rose, enthroned, to those in Antiquity
you were a calyx with one single rim.
To *us* you are the full numberless flower,
the inexhaustible thing.

Opulent rose, like robes upon robes
about a body of nothing but lustre,
each single pet yet an evasion
and a disowning of any attire.

For centuries has your fragrance been calling
its sweetest names across to us here;
it suddenly hangs like fame in the air.

Even so, we can't name it, we guess …
And recollection goes out to meet it,
granted by hours we still can re-call.

VIII

You, so few, the playmates of childhood gone by,
in gardens scattered throughout the town:
how we found and, hesitant, liked one another
and, like the Lamb with the speaking scroll,

talked in silence. When there were times we felt glad,
gladness belonged to no one. Whose was it?
And how it dwindled to nothing among all the walking people
and in the anxiety of the long year.

Carriages rolled around us, indifferent, drawn past,
houses stood round us, strong, but unreal—and none
ever knew us. What *was*, in the universe, real?

Nothing. Only the ball. Its magnificent curving flights.
Nor were the children real ... but sometimes one,
ah, one that was fading away, stepped under the falling ball.

(in memoriam Egon von Rilke)

IX

You, who give judgment, do not boast that the iron
has been unshackled from necks, and the rack dispensed with.
No heart is uplifted, not one, because a deliberate
spasm of mercy gives you a gentler twist.

What it received through the ages the scaffold
offers us back, like children the toys from their previous
birthday. Into the pure, the high, the gate-open heart
he would differently enter, the god

of genuine mercy. Mighty, he would draw near
and spread about him the radiance of gods.
More than a wind for the great assured ships.

Not less than the delicate secret awareness
which silently wins us within
like a quietly playing child of infinite pairing.

XII

Strive for transformation, O be inspired with the flame
wherein, rich in changes, a thing withdraws from your reach;
the planning spirit who masters everything earthly,
loves above all in the sweep of the figure the point where it turns.

What locks itself in endurance grows rigid; sheltered
in unassuming greyness, does it feel safe?
Wait, from the distance hardness is menaced by something still harder.
Alas—: a remote hammer is poised to strike.

Knowledge knows him who pours forth as a spring;
delighted she guides him, showing him what was created in joy
and often concludes with beginning and starts with the end.

Every happy space they traverse in wonder
is child or grandchild of parting. And Daphne, transformed,
feeling herself laurel, wants you to change into wind.

XIII

Be ahead of all parting as if it were left behind you
thus as the winter which now is going.
For there is, among winters, one so endlessly winter
that wintering through it your heart will ever prevail.

Be always dead in Eurydice—mount with more singing,
mount with more praising back into pure relation.
Here, among those who are waning, be in the realm of decline
a ringing glass that shatters in ringing.

Be—and simultaneously know the condition of not
being, the infinite source of your inmost vibration,
that you may wholly fulfil it this one single time.

The used as well as the dulled and the mute
store of plentiful Nature—untellable sums—
jubilant, join and cancel the count.

XV

O fountain-mouth, o generous mouth
which inexhaustibly continues saying
the one pure thing,—you marble mask
before the water's flowing face. Beyond,

the aqueducts' descent. From far away,
past tombs, from the Appenines' slope,
they bring to you your saying
which, past the blackened ageing of your chin,

then falls into the basin there before it.
This is the sleeping, the recumbent ear,
the ear of marble into which you always speak.

An ear of Earth's. Thus she is talking
with herself alone. And if a pitcher
slips in she feels you interrupt her.

XVII

Where, in what ever blissfully watered gardens, on what
trees, out of what calyxes tenderly stripped of their petals,
do they ripen, the strange fruits of consolation? Those,
so delicious, one of which you may find in the trampled meadow

of your poverty. Time and again you marvel
at the size of the fruit, at its being whole,
at its delicate skin, and that you had not been forestalled
by the bird's levity nor by the jealousy

of the worm below. Can it be there are trees frequented by angels
and cultivated so strangely by slow concealed gardeners
that they are bearing for us without being ours?

Have we never been able, we shadows and shades,
by our conduct—hastily ripened, and faded again—
to disturb those tranquil summers' equanimity?

XIX

Gold dwells somewhere in the pampering bank, and affects
to be on familiar terms with thousands. But the blind man,
that beggar—to even a penny he seems a desolate place,
like the corner under a cupboard covered with dust.

Money feels quite at home in the shops, and assumes
apparent disguise as silk, carnations, and furs.
Silent he stands in the pause between intakes of breath
of all that money breathing, awake or asleep.

How does it close at night, that hand perpetually open.
Tomorrow Fate will fetch it again, and each day
bring it forward: pallid, pitiful, endlessly fragile.

Would that someone, an onlooker, marvelling, finally grasped
and extolled its endurance. Only the singer could give it voice.
Only the god would hear.

XX

Between the stars, what a distance; and yet how even much
more distant
what we experience here.
One, for instance, a child ... and, next him, another—
how inconceivably far.

Fate perhaps measures us all with the span of being,
and therefore seems to us strange;
think of the many spans from girl to man only
when she both loves him and flees.

All is remote—at no point does the circle close.
Look, in the dish on a gaily laid table—
how peculiar the faces of fish.

Fishes are dumb ... one used to imagine. Who knows?
But might there not be some place where is spoken
what would be the language of fishes, *without* them?

XXI

Sing the gardens, my heart, those you have never known;
gardens as though poured in glass, clear, out of reach.
Waters and roses of Ispahan or of Shiraz,
sing them blissfully, praise them, beyond compare.

Show you are not deprived of them ever, my heart.
That it is you they are meant for, their ripening figs.
That you commune with their breezes which almost appear
transmuted into a vision among the blossoming boughs.

Avoid the erroneous belief that there are deprivations
inherent in the resolve once taken: to be!
You entered into the weave and silken thread.

With whatever image you inwardly may be united
(be it even a moment out of a life of pain)
feel that the whole, the glorious carpet is meant.

XXII

O in spite of Fate: the glorious abundances
of our existence, gushed over in parks,—
or as stone men, forced against arches of high
portals, under the balconies!

O the bell of bronze that raises its club
daily against a dull everyday.
Or the *one* in Karnak, the column, the column
outlasting almost-eternal temples.

Today the same, those surpluses, rush
past as mere speed, from yellow horizontal
day into night exaggerated with dazzling light.

But the rushing passes and leaves no traces.
Curves of the flight through the air and who flew them,
maybe none is in vain. But only as if thought.

XXIII

Call me at the one among your hours
which incessantly resists you:
like dogs' faces, suppliantly
close to you, but ever turned away

when you think at last you grasp it.
Most your own is what is thus withdrawn.
We are free. We were dismissed
where we thought we had just been received.

Anxious, we keep yearning for support,
we, at times too young for what is old
and too old for what has never been,

doing justice only when we praise
since we are the branch, ah, and the steel
and the sweetness of a danger growing ripe.

XXIV

O this delight, ever new, out of loosened loam!
Almost no one lent help to the earliest darers.
Cities rose nonetheless beside blissful gulfs,
pitchers were filled nonetheless with water and oil.

Gods,—we plan them in daring sketches
which sullen Fate again destroys.
But they are immortals. See, it is granted
our hearing to reach him who hears us at last.

We, through millenniums one lineage: mothers and fathers
ever more fulfilled with the future child
which shall, surpassing, shatter us, later.

We, so endlessly ventured, we, how much time we have!
And only taciturn Death, *he* knows what we are
and what, when he lends us, he always gains.

XXV

Listen: already, you hear the first
harrows at work; human rhythm again
amid the tense stillness of strong
early-spring earth. What is coming seems

a fresh experience again. What has come
so often, seems to be coming once more
quite new. Though hoped-for time and again,
you never seized it. It always seized you.

Even the leaves of wintered oaks
seem at sunset a future brown.
Breezes at times give each other a sign.

Bushes are black. But heaps of manure
lie on the fields, a richer black.
Each hour grows younger as it goes by.

XXVI

How it grips us, the cry of a bird …
Any cry that was once created.
But children even, at play in the open,
cry wide of genuine cries.

Crying chance cries. They drive their shrill
wedges of screaming into interstices
of space, all space (the pure bird-cry
glides in as we into dreams).

Where, alas, are we? Freer and freer,
like kites broken loose,
we chase in mid-air, with borders of laughter

slashed by the wind.—Array the criers,
singing god! that they wake, a surging
current which carries the head and the lyre.

XXVIII

O come and go. Still almost child, lend fleeting
completion to the figure of the dance,
to form as pure a constellation as those other
dances in which we transitorily surpass

dull, unimaginative Nature. For she stirred
entirely hearing only once, when Orpheus sang.
You were the one still moved from then, and slightly
bewildered when a tree took long to ponder

before it would decide to join you, hearing.
You knew the place still where the lyre, resounding,
rose—: the unimaginable centre.

It was for this you tried your lovely dance-steps
and hoped that one day you might turn your friend's
movement and face toward complete communion.

XXIX

Silent friend of every distance, feel
how your breath is still increasing space.
In the chambers of dark belfries
let yourself be rung. What wears you out

will grow strong by such food. Go
in and out in transformation.
Which experience is most painful?
If to drink is bitter, grow to wine.

Be in this night of excess
magic power at the cross-roads of your senses,
be the meaning of this strange encounter.

If forgotten by things earthly,
to the quiet earth say: I am flowing.
To the rapid water speak: I am.

PART II

from *The Book of Images*

['Whoever you may be...']

Whoever you may be: when it is evening
step from your room in which you know all things;
your own house is the last one on the edge of distance,
whoever you may be.
Then with your tired eyes which are barely able
to break free from the worn-down doorstep
you lift quite slowly a black tree and place it
against the sky: slender, alone.
And you have made the world. And it is great
and like a word that still matures in silence.
And as your will takes in its meaning
your eyes release it tenderly ...

Childhood

Drawn-out time and fear at school drag on
with nothing but dull dreary things, with waiting.
O loneliness, o weary time that will not pass …
And out at last: the streets all ring and sparkle
and there are fountains springing in the squares,
and in the parks the world becomes—so spacious.
To walk through all this in one's little suit,
walk in a way the others never walked—:
Mysterious time, o time that will not pass,
o loneliness.

To gaze at all this with a distant look:
the men and women, men, men, women
and children, colourful and distant from oneself;
and there a house, and now and then a dog,
and terror interchanging noiselessly with confidence—:
O sadness with no meaning, and o dream, o horror,
unfathomable depth.

And, in a park which softly loses colour,
to play with ball and ring and hoop,
and—blind, and savage with the headlong chase—
to brush at times against the adults;
but in the evening, silent, with small stiff
steps to be going homewards, firmly led—:
O ever more eluding comprehension,
o fear, o burden.

And by the large grey pond, to kneel
for hours with one's small sailing-boat,
and to forget it because similar
and lovelier sails move through the water's rings;
to have to think about the small
pale face which, sinking, gleamed out of the pond—:
O childhood, o fugitive images.
Where gone? Where gone?

People at Night

Nights were not made for the crowd.
Night parts your neighbour from you
and you shall not endeavour to find him.
And if at night you look up from your room
to look into people's faces
you have to consider: whose.

People are grossly disfigured
by light trickling down their faces,
and if they have flocked together at night
you see a tottering world,
piled up in confusion.
A yellow gleam on their brows has displaced
all thought, their glances flicker with wine,
from their hands there hang the heavy gestures
by which they understand
each other when they speak;
and they keep on saying: I, and I,
and meaning: Anyone.

Anxiety

There is a bird-cry in the wilting wood
which, in this wilting wood, appears to hold no meaning.
And yet it rests, the round cry of a bird,
—wide like a sky upon the wilting wood—
within this span of time that has created it.
And everything glides pliantly into the cry.
Soundless, the whole land seems to lie in it,
the great wind seems to nestle into it,
the minute anxious to move on
is pale and quiet as though it had knowledge
of things that would make everybody die, who had
emerged from the cry.

['Loneliness is like...']

Loneliness is like a rain.
It rises from the sea to meet the evenings;
from plains far distant, it sets out
to reach the sky which never is without it.
And from the sky it then falls on the town.

Raining downwards in the hours of twilight
when all streets are turning towards the morning
and when bodies which found nothing,
sad and disenchanted, let each other go,
and when people full of hatred for each other
have to sleep together in one bed,

loneliness flows with the rivers ...

Autumn Day

Lord: it is time. The summer was so great.
You rest your shadow on the sun-dials,
and in the meadows release the winds.

Command the last fruits to be full;
grant them yet two more southern-days
and urge them towards perfection, chase
sweetness into heavy wine.

Who has no house now will not build one.
Who is alone will long remain so,
will wake, and read, and write long letters,
and restlessly pace up and down
the avenues, among the drifting leaves.

Evening

The evening slowly changes robes
held ready by a border of old trees;
you gaze: the lands are passing from you,
one rises skywards and the other falls;

and leave you who belongs to neither wholly,
not quite so darkened as the mute house,
not quite so sure in your appeal to the eternal
as that which turns into a star to rise at night—

and leave to you (how hard to unravel)
your life, immense, uneasy and maturing,
which—now restricted, and now full of insight—
becomes a stone or constellation.

Fragments from Lost Days

... Like birds which have become accustomed
to walking and grow heavier, as in falling:
the earth sucks out of their long claws
the brave remembrance of those many
great things that happen high above
and turns them almost into leaves, to hold them
close to the ground,—
like plants
which, scarcely growing upwards, creep into the earth,
sink down into black clods and pine away,
lifelessly bright and soft and damp,
like insane children,—like a face
inside a coffin,—like happy hands
that grow irresolute because in the full cup
things are reflected that are not nearby,
like cries for help that in the evening wind
meet many large dark bells,—
like flowers in a room, for days kept dry,
like streets of bad repute,—like curls
among which precious stones turned blind,—
like April mornings
before the many windows of the hospital:
the sick all crowd the same side of the hall
and gaze: the mercy of an early sun-beam
makes all the streets seem wide and spring-like;
they only see bright splendour
that makes the houses young with laughter,
and do not know that all the night
a storm has torn the coverings off the skies,
a storm of waters, with the world still bound by ice,
a storm still rushing through the streets
and taking all the burden off things' shoulders,—
that outside there is something vast and furious,
that outside there goes violence, a fist,
that it would strangle each one of the sick
amidst this radiance in which they believe.

... Like long nights inside withered arbours
already torn apart on every side
and far too large for anyone to weep
in them with one he dearly loves,—
like naked maidens walking over stones,
like drunk men in a birch-tree grove,—
like words which have no definite meaning
and yet pass on, pass on into the ear and, farther,
into the brain, and secretly—along the ladder
of nerves—try leap by leap through all the limbs.
Like old men cursing at their sex, and then
passing away so that none ever could
avert the woe imposed on them,—
like roses in full bloom, reared artificially
in the blue hothouse where the false breezes told untruths,
and then, in a large curve, by wantonness
scattered across the drifted snow,—
and like a planet unable to revolve
because too many dead weigh down its feeling,
and like a slain man, buried carelessly,
whose hands defend themselves against the roots,—
like one of those tall, slender, red
midsummer flowers, dying suddenly,
without fulfilment, in the meadows' favourite wind
because its root below
strikes
against turquoises in a dead woman's ear-ring ...

Thus were the hours of certain days. As if
somebody somewhere moulded my image
slowly to torture it with pins.
Conscious of each sharp point of his sport
I felt as if a rain fell down on me
in which all things pass through a change.

from *The Book of Hours*

['To you, my praying ...']

To you, my praying is no blasphemy,
as though I found confirmed in ancient books
my close and thousandfold relation to you.

.... I want to give you love in various ways.

But does one love one's father? Does one not
—like you who left me, hardness in your face—
go forth and leave his helpless empty hands?
Does one not softly put his withered word
into old books one seldom reads?
Does one not flow off from his heart,
as from a water-shed, to joy and sorrow?
Is not a father what has been
the years gone by with unfamiliar thought,
the dated gesture and the dead attire,
and withered hands and faded hair?
And even if in his own time he was a hero,
he is the leaf that, when we grow, must fall.

And his solicitude is like a mountain,
his voice is like a stone,—we want
to give obedient hearing to his speech,
and yet we only half hear all his words.
The loud great drama between him and us
drowns with its noise our mutual understanding,
we merely see the outlines of his mouth
producing syllables that fall and fade away.
Thus we are farther still than far from him
though love may closely interweave us yet;
and only when he has to die upon this star
are we aware he lived upon this star.

Such is a father, to us, I—and I
should call you father? It would mean to part
a thousand times from you. You are my Son.
And I shall know you as one knows
one's own most precious child, and even when
he has become a man, an aged man.

['You are the heir …']

You are the heir.
Sons are the heirs when fathers die.
Sons stand and blossom.
      You are the heir.
And you inherit the verdure
of by-gone gardens, and the tranquil blue
of fallen skies,
dew of a thousand days,
the many summers told by suns,
and all the springs with sparkle and complaint
like a young woman's many letters.
And you inherit lying stored autumns
like robes of state within the memory of poets;
all winters seem like orphaned lands
to nestle softly close to you.
And you inherit Venice and Kazan and Rome,
Florence will be your own, Pisa's Cathedral,
the Troitzka Lavra, and the Monastir
that forms a maze of corridors,
dark and entangled, under Kiev's gardens,—
Moscow with bells like memories,—
sound will be yours: horns, violins and tongues,
and every song that rang profound enough
will shine, a precious stone, on you.

For you alone the poets seek seclusion
and garner rich and rushing images,
and they go forth and, by comparing, grow mature
and are their whole lives all alone.
For you the painters only paint their pictures
and garner, as permanent,
Nature you made impermanent: all things
become eternal. Woman has long been
mature like wine in Mona Lisa;
never again should there be any woman
for no new woman adds anything new.
And sculptors are like you. They want
eternity. And they say: stone
be eternal and that means: be yours!

Those, too, who love are garnering for you:
they are the poets of a transient hour,
they kiss a smile upon a passive mouth
as though to give it a more lovely form,
they bring keen pleasure and they teach us pains
that will transform us into adults.
And with their laughter they bring sorrows,
longings that are asleep, but waken
to weep aloud within the unfamiliar breast.
They pile up mysteries and die
as beasts die, without comprehension,—
but it may be they will have grandsons
in whom their green lives grow to ripeness:
through these you will inherit love
those gave each other blind, as though asleep.
This superabundance of things flows to you.
And as the upper basin of a fountain
constantly overflows, as though from tresses
of loosened hair, into the lowest bowl—
thus fullness falls into your valleys
when things and thoughts flow over.

['I'm merely one…']

I'm merely one of your most humble servants
who, more remote from people than from things,
looks out at life from his monastic cell
not daring to evaluate what happens.
But if you summoned me before your face
in which, all dark, your eyes are raised
do not regard that I presume too much
if I should tell you: No one lives his life.
People are chances, voices, fragments,
everydays, fears, and many little blisses,
disguised when children, wrapped in many wraps,
eloquent masks, but reticent faces.

I often think: there must be treasure houses
in which these many lives lie stored
like suits of armour, cradles or sedan chairs
never yet used by real living man,
like robes that cannot by themselves alone
stand upright and, in sinking, nestle closely
against strong walls of curving stone.
And if I went on walking in the evening
out of my garden I am weary in—
I know that every road would lead to
the arsenal of un-lived things.
There is no tree in the recumbent landscape,
and windowless, as though to guard a prison,
the wall describes a circle sevenfold.
And all its gates with iron bolts
  —to keep out all who want to enter—
and all its bars were made by man.

['Now the red rowans…']

Now the red rowans are already ripening
and ageing asters faintly breathe in flower-beds.
Who is not rich now that the summer goes
will wait and never be entirely his own self.

Who is not able *now* to close his eyes,
quite certain that a multitude of images
is only waiting in him till the night begins,
and then to rise within his darkness:
is gone like an old man.

And nothing more will come to him, no day occurs
and everything that happens lies to him,
you, too, my God. And you are like a stone
you daily draw him down into the deep.

['God, have no fear ...']

God, have no fear. They keep on saying: mine
of every patient thing.
They are like wind that grazes boughs
and says: *my* tree.

They barely feel
how everything their hands grasp, glows—
they cannot, without burning, hold it,
not even by its very fringe.

They keep on saying *mine* as, in a talk with peasants,
one likes to call the Sovereign one's friend
when he is very great and—very distant.
They keep on saying *mine* about their unknown walls
and do not know the master of their house.
They keep on saying *mine* and call their property
all things that close when they draw near—
thus as a common charlatan
might speak of sun and lightning as his own.
And thus they say: my life, my wife,
my dog, my child, and yet they know full well
that everything: life, wife and dog and child
are unknown forms they knock against
with hands stretched forward, blind.
This is a certainty to no one but the great
who long for eyes. The others do not want
to hear that their warm wandering
has no connection with the things around them
and, forced away from their belongings
and not acknowledged by their property,
they *own* a woman no more than a flower
that has a life unknown to all.

God, do not lose your equanimity.
He, too, who loves you and who recognizes
your face in darkness when, like candle-light,
he sways within your breath—does not possess you.
If someone grasps you in the night
and forces you into his prayer:
                    You are the Guest
                         who passes on.

God, who can hold you? You are all your own,
by no possessor's hand disturbed,
as wine that has not reached maturity
and goes on growing sweeter, is its own.

['I dig for you …']

I dig for you, the treasure, in deep nights.
For all the riches I have ever seen
are poverty and paltry substitute
for your own beauty never yet revealed
…

I hold my open hands which bleed
with digging, out into the wind
and there they branch out like a tree.
And with my hands I draw you out of space
as though, in an impatient gesture,
you had once dashed yourself to fragments there
and now you fell, a shattered world,
from far-off stars upon the earth
as softly as the rain falls in the spring.

['… Lord, the large cities …']

… Lord, the large cities are
doomed and divided;
the largest is like flight from flames,—
there is no consolation to console it,
its span of time is running out.

There people live a hard exacting life
in basements, fearful of a gesture,
more frightened than a herd of yearlings are;
outside there is your wakeful breathing earth,
but they exist, and do not know it any more.

There children grew up near the window-ledges
that are forever in the self-same shadow,
and do not know that, outside, flowers call to
a day of space and happiness and wind,—
meant to be children they are, sadly, children.

There virgins blossom out to the unknown
and they keep yearning for their childhood's peace;
but what they burn for is not there
and, trembling, they close again.
And pass in closely curtained back-rooms
the days of disappointed motherhood,
the long-drawn-out nights of helpless moans,
and cold years with no strength nor struggle.
And there are death-beds, standing in the dark,
and they approach them slowly in their yearning
and take a long time dying, dying as in chains,
and end like beggar-women.

There people live in pallid bloom
and, puzzled, die of the exacting world.
And no one notices the gaping
grimace to which the smile of such a gentle people
twists in unimaginable nights.

They move about, degraded by the toil
of listless servitude to things that could hold no meaning;

their garments fade on them, and their hands
—once beautiful—grow prematurely old.

The crowd keep pressing onward with no thought
of sparing them, the hesitant and weak,—
and only timid dogs that have no place to live in
walk quietly behind them for a while.

Abandoned to a hundred torturers,
shouted at by every striking of the hour,
they circle, lonely, round the hospitals
and, fearfully, kept waiting for Admission Day.

And there is Death. But not the same whose message
had touched them wondrously in childhood,—
the little death they had then understood;
their own death, green and with no sweetness,
hangs in them like a fruit that will not ripen.

O Lord, grant each one his own death,
such dying grant him as would issue from
a life in which he once had love and need and meaning.

We merely are the rind and leaf.
The great death each one has within himself—
that is the fruit around which everything revolves.

['Lord, we are poorer …']

Lord, we are poorer than poor beasts
(they end, though blind, with their own death)
because, as yet, we none of us have died.
Him give us, him who gains the knowledge
of tying Life up to espaliers round which
May has an earlier beginning.

Dying is hard and unfamiliar:
it is not our own death; at last it takes us
because we have not ripened death ourselves;
and thus there goes a storm to strip us off.

We stand within your garden, year by year,
and are the trees to bear sweet death;
but we grow old on harvest-days;
and thus as women whom you blighted,
we are all bad and closed and barren.

Or is my self-conceit unjust:
perhaps the trees are better? Are we merely sex,
and womb of women who grant much?—
We have been whoring with Eternity,
And when we reach the bed of labour
we bear the dead miscarriage of our death;
the sorrowful and crooked embryo
who (as if something frightful frightened him)
hides in his hands his rudiments of eyes,
and on whose towering brow
there is already the fear of what he did not suffer,—
and all end like a bulging whore convulsed in labour
and undergoing a caesarean.

from *Uncollected and Later Poems (1912–1926)*

Apparition

What, today, compels your return
to the restlessly rustling garden
through which, a moment ago,
there sped a shower of sunlight?
See all the green growing grave in its wake.
Come! that I might, like you,
disregard the weight of the trees.
(If one of them were to fall
across the path, one would have to
call for men to lift it. What is,
in the world, as heavy?)
The many stone steps
you descended more loudly: I heard you.
Now you again make no sound.
I am alone in hearing,
with myself, with the wind ... On a sudden
a nightingale sings
in the sheltered thicket.
Hear, in the air, how the towering song
stands crumbling or not completed.
Are you listening with me,—
or does even now the other side of the voice,
which turns away from us, keep you preoccupied?

['Pearls roll down ...']

Pearls roll down. Alas, did one of the strings break?
But of what avail would it be if I strung them again:
I need you, beloved, strong clasp, to retain them.

Is it not time? As the dawn for the sunrise,
I am waiting for you, pale with the night overcome;
like a crowded theatre I form a large face
that nothing of your high central appearance
should escape me. O as a gulf hopes into the open
and throws, from the upright lighthouse,
shining spaces; as, in the desert, a river-bed hopes
for rain to gush, still heavenly, from the pure mountains,—
as the prisoner longs, erect, for the one star's
answer into his guiltless window;
as one who tears off his warm
crutches to have them hung on the altar,
lies there and, without a miracle, cannot get up:
see, thus I twist and turn, if you do not come, till the end.

I desire only you. Must not the crack in the pavement
when, indigent, feeling the pressure of grass: must it not want
the whole spring, the spring of the earth? And does not the moon
need the strange constellation's large appearance,
for its reflection to be in the village pond?
How could the least ever happen if fullness of future,
all complete time, was not moving to meet us?

Are you not in it at last, you, the ineffable? Still a while,
and I shall no longer be able to stand the test of you.
I shall grow old or be displaced by children ...

from The Spanish Trilogy

I

Out of that cloud, see, which so wildly hides
the star which just has been—(and out of me),
out of that mountainous stretch of land which now
has night and night winds for a while—(and out of me),
out of that river in the valley down below which catches
the gleam of a torn sky-clearing—(and out of me);
out of all those, and me, to make one single thing,
Lord: out of me and of the feeling
with which the flock, returned into the pen,
resigns itself, while slowly breathing out,
to that great dark no-longer-being of the world,—
of me and every light within the dense
darkness of all those many houses, Lord:
to make one thing; out of those strangers
for, Lord, there is not one I know, and me and me
to make *one* thing; out of the people sleeping,
the unknown aged men up at the hospice
who cough importantly in bed, and out of children
heavy with sleep at unknown women's breasts,
out of the many that are undefined, and always me,
of nothing else but me and what I do not know,
to make the thing, Lord Lord Lord, the thing
which cosmic-earthly like a meteor,
its heaviness the gathered sum of flight,
weighs nothing but arrival.

II

Why must one go and take upon oneself
things that are not one's own concern, as does the porter
who lifts the market basket being filled by strangers
from stall to stall, and follows burdened
and cannot put the question: Master, why the banquet?

Why must one stand there like a shepherd—
so much exposed to the excess of influence,
so much involved in this space full of happening,
he would fulfil his destiny by doing nothing more
than lean against a tree out in the landscape.
And yet, in his far too wide gaze, he does not have
the quiet moderation of the flock. He has
nothing but world, has world in every glance he raises,
in every bending—world. What readily belongs to others
penetrates unyieldingly like music, blindly,
into his blood and, changing, passes on.

He rises in the night and has already
the bird's call in his being, and feels bold
because he gathers all the stars into his vision,
laboriously,—o not at all like someone
who spreads this night before the one he loves
and lavishes on her the heavens he has felt.

A Spring

(Paris)

O all these April dead,
the blackness of the hearses which convey them
through this excited and exaggerated light:
as if, once more, weight sullenly rebelled
against increasing lightness in all things ...
But there already those who yesterday still wore
their pinafores, surprisedly grown-up
are going to their First Communion;
their white is eager as before God's throne
and softened in the first shade of the elms.

Christ's Descent into Hell

Painless at last, his being escaped the terrible
body of sufferings. Above. Left it.
And darkness, alone, was afraid
and flung at the pallor
bats,—in the evenings, fear of collision
with anguish grown cold
still reels in their flutter. Dark restless air
grew discouraged on the dead body: obtuseness, reluctance,
was in the strong vigilant beasts of the night.
His spirit, released, perhaps meant to stand
in the landscape, inactive. For the event of his suffering
was still enough. Full of measure
seemed to him the night-presence of things,
he spread like a sorrowful space above it.
But earth, dried up in the thirst of his wounds,
but earth tore open, and something called in the abyss.
He, knower of tortures, heard Hell
howling hither, demanding consciousness
of his concluded anguish: that above termination of his
(infinite) her continuous pain should be terrified, feel it
in anticipation. And he, the spirit, plunged with the whole
weight of his exhaustion into it: strode, hurrying
through startled glances of pasturing shadows gazing
after him, raised to Adam his glance, hurriedly,
hurried down, vanished, gleamed and faded in precipices
of wilder depths. Suddenly (higher, higher), above
the centre of surging cries, on the long
tower of his suffering, he emerged: without breath
stood, without a railing, owner of pains, mute.

['Behind the guiltless trees...']

Behind the guiltless trees,
slowly, old Ill-Fate
fashions her silent face.
Wrinkles are moving across ...
What a bird screeches here
springs as a line of pain
from the hard sooth-saying mouth.

Oh, and the soon-to-be lovers
smile at each other, as yet with no knowledge of parting.
Above them there sets and rises,
like constellations, their destiny,
night-inspired.
Not yet offering itself to them as experience,
it still remains
poised in the heavens' courses,
an airy configuration.

The Great Night

Often, gazing in wonder at you, I stood at the window begun
the day before, stood as I gazed in wonder at you. The new city
was still denying me access, the unpersuaded landscape
darkened as though I did not exist. Nor did the things close at hand
endeavour to be comprehensible. Pressing forward, the street
reached up by the lamp outside: I saw it was unfamiliar.
Over there, a room, communicating its nearness, clear in the lamplight,—
I responded already; they sensed it, and closed the shutters.
I stood. Then a child cried. I knew, in the houses around,
the presence of mothers, and their resources, —and knew
also the causes beyond any solace that are at the root of all weeping.
Or a voice sang out and passed a little beyond expectation,
or, down below, there coughed an old man
full of reproach as though his body were in the right
against a gentler world. Then a clock struck the hour,—
but I counted too late, it fell past me.—
As a boy, a stranger, at last allowed to join in
yet unable to catch the ball and knowing none of the games
which the others so easily play together,
stands there, looks away—where?—I stood, and suddenly
realised *you* befriended me, played with me, grown-up
Night, and I gazed in wonder at you. While towers
were wrathful and, with its fate unrevealed,
a city stood round me, and undivinable mountains
barred my way and, in narrowing circles,
hungering strangeness encompassed the random
flickering of my feelings: there, lofty Night,
it was not shameful for you to know me. Your breath
swept across me. Your smile, dispersed over such
gravities, passed into me.

[‴One must die
because one knows them‴]

'One must die because one knows them.' Die
of the smile's ineffable blossom. Die
of their light hands. Die
of women.

Youth shall sing them, the deadly
when high-up they move through his heart-space.
Out of his blossoming breast
he shall sing them:
unattainable. Ah, how unfamiliar they are.
Above the summits
of his emotion they come forth and effuse
sweetly-transformed night in the deserted
vale of his arms. Wind of their rise
rustles in the foliage of his body.
His brooks run sparkling.

But the grown man,
more deeply harrowed, shall be mute.
He who has, pathless, strayed in the night
on the mountain-ranges of his emotions:
be mute.
As the older seaman is mute,
the mastered horrors
playing in him as in quivering cages.

['Beloved ...']

Beloved,
lost in advance, you who never appeared,
I do not know what notes you are fond of.
Not any more, with the future in ceaseless motion,
do I endeavour to recognize you. All those great
images in me, far-away landscapes fully experienced,
towns and towers and bridges and un-
expected turnings of paths
and the power of those lands
once intergrown with the lives of gods:
mount up in me to the meaning
of you who elude me.

Ah, you are the gardens,
ah, I saw them with such
hope. An open window
in a country–house, —and you almost stepped
pensively towards me. I came upon streets
down which you had just been walking,
and sometimes the mirrors in dealers' shops
were still dizzy with you and, startled, returned
my too sudden reflection. Who knows if the same
bird was not singing perhaps through us both,
separately, yesterday evening.

['Exposed on the hills …']

Exposed on the hills of the heart. See, how small there,
see: the last hamlet of words and, higher,
but how small too, yet a last
farmstead of feeling. There, can you glimpse it?
Exposed on the hills of the heart. Stone ground
under one's hands. Still, there is here
something that blossoms; out of the soundless precipice
there sings an unknowing herb as it blossoms forth.
But he who knows? ah, he who began to know
and now is silent, exposed on the hills of the heart.
With an undivided awareness, many a creature
wanders there still, many a sure
mountain beast roams and remains. Secure, the great bird
circles the peaks' pure rejection.—But
vulnerable here on the hills of the heart …

['Again and again …']

Again and again, although we know the landscape of love
and the little churchyard with its plaintive names
and the terribly silent ravine where the others
end: again and again we go out two together
beneath the old trees, lie down again and again
among the flowers, face to face with the sky.

['Music: breathing of statues …']

Music: breathing of statues. Perhaps
stillness of paintings. Languages where languages
end; time
standing, vertical, on the direction of waning hearts.

Feelings for whom? O you, transformation of feelings,
into what? into audible landscape.
O stranger: music. Heart-space
that has outgrown us. Most intimately our own
which, transcending us, surging away from us—sacred parting:
we being surrounded by what is within,
as most practised remoteness, the other
side of the air,
pure,
immense,
no longer inhabitable.

['When catching what you throw' ...]

When catching what you throw yourself, it all
is mere dexterity, dispensable attainment;
only when all at once you catch the ball
which she, eternal fellow-player,
has flung to you, your centre, with a throw
exactly mastered, in an arc like those
of God's great bridges: only then
ability to catch becomes achievement—
not yours, a world's. And if you even
had strength and courage to return the ball,
no, still more wonderful: forgot both strength and courage
and *had* already thrown it, ... as the year
throws birds, the swarms of migratory birds
an older warmth hurls far across the seas
to young, new warmth,—then only, in such daring,
you play at last a valid part.
You make the throw no longer easier for yourself,
no longer harder for yourself. Out of your hands,
a meteor hurtles on its course through space ...

Imaginary Life

First, childhood, boundless, with no aim,
no renunciation. O unconscious bliss!
Abruptly, terror, limits, school and bondage,
and headlong falling to temptation and to loss.

Defiance. He who had been bent bends others—
inflicts, on others, vengeance for his own defeat.
Loved, feared, he rescues, wrestles, wins
and overcomes, with rapid blow on blow.

Alone, a weightless cold expanse about him.
But deep within his upright body he draws breath
now that the first, the old deed has been done ...

Then God rushed forward from His ambush.

The Magician

He calls it up. It gives a start, and stands.
What stands? The other; all that is not him
grows being. The whole being turns
a rapidly-made face round that is more.

Magician, o prevail, prevail, prevail!
Create an equipoise. Stand quietly upon the scales
that they may bear you and the house
on one side and that augmentation on the other.

Decision falls. Connection is produced.
He knows, the call outweighed refusal.
But—like a clock with meeting hands—
his face has midnight. He is also bound.

Appendix

Note to *Selected Poems* (1942)

What I have aimed at is to give as exact a translation as is humanly possible. I have tried in the case of each poem to keep to the original metre, but I have made no attempt at rhymed verse because a rhyme coming naturally and necessarily in the one language would have to be forced in the translation—and much of the original text would have to be sacrificed or mutilated merely for the sake of rhyme. Rilke's abundance of meaning does not *depend* on rhyme for its transmission, but bursts upon us in some degree even through a 'prose' translation if only we let him speak in words that, in the kindred language, are as closely equivalent to his own as it is possible to render them.

I have been led to attempt to render Rilke in English because I regard him as a great European poet—one of the two or three, perhaps, of our century (he lived from 1875 to 1926).

I should like to use this opportunity for expressing sincere thanks to John Speirs, Terence Tiller and Bernard Spencer who have taken an active interest in my translations and have given me valuable suggestions for which I am grateful.

Ruth Speirs [undated]

Unsigned *Times Literary Supplement* reviews by Ruth Speirs

The following unsigned Ruth Speirs reviews in the *Times Literary Supplement* are offered as illustration of her views on the translation of Rilke's poetry.

29 November 1957
['Rilke without music': *Poems 1906 to 1926*. Translated by J. B. Leishman. Hogarth Press]

Rilke never ceased regretting the fact that he had leaped into print while his work was still immature, and during the last two decades of his life he became increasingly averse from publication. Thus arose the legend that he had been incapable of writing poetry from the inception of the *Duino Elegies* in 1912 until their completion in 1922, although the verse written during those years fills some 130 pages. Some of these poems have remained fragmentary, some were so personal that Rilke did not wish to divulge them, others again were written for friends and presented to them, while several of the complete poems appeared in reviews and were not available in book form. In 1953 the Insel-Verlag published the vast material on which Professor Ernst Zinn had been working since 1937, comprising all the poems Rilke wrote in German after 1906, with the exception of the *Duino Elegies*, the *Sonnets to Orpheus*, *From the Remains of Count C. W.* and the *Correspondence in Verse with Erika Mitterer*.

This collection is now available in English in the translation of Mr J. B. Leishman; he has set out the poems in chronological sequence, a method which is less confusing for the reader than Professor Zinn's original arrangement, which consists of three parts divided into sub-sections. However, one cannot help feeling that it would have been an advantage for those who wish to compare the original with the translation if the poems had been set out in the same sequence, so that one might read them in both languages without having to look up the letters and page numbers which follow the index of titles and first lines.

It is regrettable indeed that the sheer length of the work precluded the possibility of printing original and translation on opposite pages, for no one who does not refer to the German text can gain even a shadowy idea of Rilke's greatness as a poet. Unfortunately the old adage 'traduttore—traditore' holds good in nearly every case when someone who is not a poet attempts to re-create poetry in another language, and it is little short of a tragedy that verses by the poet who made the German language sing, using it with a subtle mastery that is unique, expressing hitherto unknown shades of emotion with absolute precision and making of every line a gem of rhythmical perfection, should be transcribed in a manner devoid of the essential qualities of poetry. One example may suffice. Where Rilke exclaims:

Heil mir, das ich Ergriffene sehe. Schon lange
war uns das Schauspiel nicht wahr
und das erfundene Bild sprach nicht entscheidend uns an.

we find the flat, prosaic lines:

Oh, to see men in the grip of something! Already
our drama had grown unreal,
and the invented image no longer answered our hearts.

Admittedly, there is no English equivalent for the ecstatic 'Heil mir', but surely 'Ergriffene' might have been rendered more adequately by a reference to emotion; also, Rilke does not say that the drama itself had become unreal, but that it seemed unreal to us.

Sometimes Mr Leishman succeeds unexpectedly in singing in the very tone and mode of the original, as in the early poem "Song" from *The Notebooks of Malte Laurids Brigge*, but this is rather an exception than a rule. The sheer industry and concentration with which he has carried out this task commands respect. However, one can only hope that the interest in Rilke will continue until, at some future date, several poets, fired by the kind of enthusiasm that urged Rilke himself to re-write some of Valéry's finest poems in his own language, will unite in their efforts to give us a less distorted reflection of the beauty by which he enriched the world.

28 July 1961
['The Language of Rilke'. (A commentary on 'recent efforts to
present Rilke to the English-speaking public': Eudo C. Mason,
Rilke, Europe and the English-Speaking World, Cambridge
University Press, 1961; Romano Guardini, *Rilke's Duino Elegies*,
tr. by K. G. Knight, Darwen Finlayson, 1961; *The Book of Hours*,
tr. by A. L. Peck, with an introduction by Eudo C. Mason,
Hogarth Press, 1961)]

[...] Professor Mason, in an introduction [to A L Peck's version
of *The Book of Hours*] convincingly analyses Rilke's attitude to
God in *The Book of Hours*, Rilke's conception of God as the final
product and not the first cause of the cosmic process, and his
conception of art as playing an essential role in bringing God
into existence. Dr Peck states in his preface:

> From the first I determined that the only translation worth
> producing would be one [...] in some degree capable of
> taking the place of the original [...] capable of conveying
> [...] a true impression of the qualities of the original [...] My
> aim, therefore, has been a high one.

This is the first complete translation of Rilke's *Stunden-
Buch*, and readers with insufficient knowledge of German
have nothing at all with which to compare it. Dr Peck has
taken a great responsibility upon himself. Unfortunately his
translation cannot be said—even 'in some degree'—to take the
place of the original or to give a true impression of its qualities.

In the *Stunden-Buch* itself all is simplicity and ease, the lines
flow effortlessly (Professor Mason speaks of the 'flux of its sweet,
seductive cadences'), the language is simple and economical. In
the translation, all is strain and verbosity. Though Dr Peck tries
to keep to the original, Rilke's melodious and delicate poetry is
drowned in the translator's desperate straining for rhyme, his
unfortunate choice of words, and his continual inversion of the
English word order, to force rhyme that otherwise would not
come (yet he says: 'In particular, the translator must never let
rhyme [...] hold an absolute domination [...]'). Books I and II
are especially bad.

Such lines as 'Why fail my hands at brushwork?', 'Comes for
your building, God, a novice hither', 'and thought once more

your brows deep knit', 'abroad the whispering rumours creep'
are absurd, but comprehensible. Yet what of the following:

> Before that time born judgment's rays
> my visage bowed saw—that which sways
> its speech thenceforth—your form
> on me and on the whole world's face …?

And what has become of Rilke's 'sweet, seductive cadences'?

> See you not how my soul before you here,
> in dress of silent stillness clad, stands close?
> Fragrance your smooth branches forth are sending.
> And you ask not if still wake my eyes …

One could fill pages with similar quotations.
  Dr Peck says that it is

> a primary duty of the translator never himself to introduce
> anything unconvincing where there is nothing in the
> original to justify him: and this is a principle which applies
> not only to individual words and formulations of words but
> also to phrases and modes of expression.

'Unconvincing' is a vague term; anything might 'convince' a
reader who cannot read the original. But what about 'where
there is nothing in the original to justify him'? Is Dr Peck
justified in translating *bange* or *bang* (anxious, uneasy, afraid),
one of the key words in all Rilke's poetry, as *distressed*, *terrified*,
astounded (twice), *scared for fear*, *bodings grey*? Where Rilke is all
simplicity, is the translator justified in being turgid? Here are a
few examples; a literal translation is in parentheses:

> 'He that with boasting's vain protesting
> Swore he'd all winged fowl outfly'
> (he who presumed to outdo all birds in flying)
> 'and in your presence takes its station
> as't were the tallest of the angel-nation'
> (and stands before you like the tallest of all angels)
> 'whose desore's by narrowest limits bounded'

(who ask for nothing)
'whose will's but a blank'
(they want nothing)
'their cry there's no denying'
(they cry)
'nor fret nor flown'
(willingly)
'he would figure clear'
(he would see)

A 'circle' becomes *some region small*, 'differently' becomes *far otherwise*, 'many'—*exceeding manifold*, 'often'—*amain and oftentimes*.

Dr Peck frequently embellishes his translation not only by altering the original but also by adding to it. Rilke's beasts become 'dumb and drear', a peasant becomes 'rough ungroomly', the law of gravity is given a 'greedy paw', and Rilke's 'Go, break the bells' becomes 'Off, smash your bells with bangs and blows!' He even introduces a governess ('so taught his governess') where Rilke has *women*. But worse is to come; one can scarcely believe it, but Rilke's 'ears of the dead' have become

ears that know no wise notion.

It is enough to make the reader feel like the person in Dr Peck's translation:

resigned and glum, of revellings desolate.

28 May 1964
['Rilke in an alien tongue'. *New Poems*. The German Text,
with a Translation, Introduction and Notes by J. B. Leishman.
Hogarth Press]

This translation of all the poems in the two collections *Neue Gedichte* (1907) and *Der Neuen Gedichte andere Teil* (1908) was completed before J. B. Leishman's death, and it seems that it would have concluded his work as translator of Rilke's major collections even if he had not died prematurely last year. The Introduction and notes are at once enthusiastic and well-informed, showing that, thanks to the translator's active involvement in his texts, Leishman's long familiarity with Rilke was immune to the contempt that has tended to infect all but the most devoted of Rilke's critics. As a translator, Leishman could remain closely identified with his poet to the last. As a translator, too, he was less tempted than the critics to divert his attention from Rilke's admirable craftsmanship to his personal foibles and absurdities.

Regrettably, though, the same self-identification led Leishman into foibles and absurdities that could easily discredit not Rilke's person, but his work. Whatever he says in the Introduction—and this contains some excellent insights into Rilke's work, especially into the nature of the *Dinggedicht* or 'thing-poem' to which he turned in these two collections under the influence of Rodin and Cézanne, as a deliberate counter-measure to the pseudo-mystical subjectivity of the *Stunden-Buch*. Leishman must have thought of Rilke as a mannerist in poetry as well as in life. It is true, of course, that Rilke imposed his peculiar sensibility on the German language, to the extent of neologism, where necessary, and of daring grammatical, syntactical and stylistic innovation throughout. Yet he was also a master of the vernacular, of simple and natural speech—an element no less essential to his work than to Yeats or Mr Pound or Mr Eliot.

It could be, too, that the fault lay less in the incompleteness of Leishman's self-identification with Rilke than in his sense of poetic diction and prosody in general. In the Introduction he provides a translation of Baudelaire's 'La Charogne', somewhat gratuitously perhaps, but with an eagerness and enthusiasm rare enough in our time to be charming and touching. Disturbingly, though, this version shows the same mannerisms, especially in the rhyming, as Leishman's renderings of Rilke (e.g. the rhyming of 'loathsomeness' with 'consciousness', *'thence-*/forth' with 'quintessence').

What is certain and inescapable is that Leishman's versions of these poems torment and violate the English language in a way that was not Rilke's with the German language. On the very first page the poem 'Girls Lament' contains three instances: the nouns 'self-withdrawingness' and 'comprehendingness'— perpetrated for a rhyme, as so often—and the misleading 'outhounded', used in the sense of 'hounded out'. The original, 'Mädchenklage' is quite innocent of such distortions, as 'Der Junggeselle' is of the obscure and cumbersome:

> and he was consubstantiated
> with his own kin, who now with him outdied.

Here Leishman cannot have meant 'died out', as the analogy of 'outhounded' would suggest, since Rilke says only that he 'became fused with this kin'.

Not even a rhyme—and Rilke's rhyming was masterly in its fluency and its capacity to set up an organic relation between sound and sense—materializes from the clumsy acrobatics of these lines from "Sappho to Alcaeus":

> I the seer and all those who've been il-
> lumined by me, to a god's delight,—

and nowhere does Rilke's diction create any precedent for contractions like:

> what in you, though, 's had beginning

or, much worse,

> and in old blue note-paper, ther're traces

especially in view of the fact that Leishman's scansion is irregular and eccentric enough to accommodate the odd syllable.

The rhyming of adverbs like 'spoilingly' and 'disturbingly', or 'seekingly' and 'furtively', as on noun and participle suffixes, like 'never-credited' and 'unparented' becomes monotonous and obtrusive and grate[s] unmercifully on the ear. Sometimes the rhyming is quite unrelated to the kind of sound effects which Rilke's poems convey. Who would guess, for instance, that the original of

> like serpents terribly abashing
> her naked arms stretch out aroused and gnashing

enacts not only the serpentine movements of the Spanish dancer's arms, but also the rattling of castanets?

Rilke's small girl on the Paris merry-go-round becomes 'a little maiden'—changed, changed utterly by that little transposition into a creature of coy fiction. Rilke's 'abgenommener Baum' in 'David Singt vor Saul' is not an 'amputated tree', but merely a tree whose fruit has been picked. If this is a case of simple mistranslation, far more often Leishman's grotesqueries are deliberate and inexplicable. One instance is the use of abstract nouns and abstract constructions; Leishman not only faithfully renders Rilke's—and German, notoriously, is more given to abstraction than English—but succeeds in creating new ones where Rilke has taken care to be concrete. His beautifully simple line

> Wunden schlägt mir dein Flügelschlag

becomes

> I'm bruised by the beat of your winged away—

and totally incomprehensible.

The only translations quite free from mannered doggerel are those of poems in blank verse, such as the magnificent *Orpheus. Eurydice. Hermes.* Leishman's rendering of this can bear comparison not only with the best of his earlier Rilke versions, but with renderings of the same poem by other translators, not excluding Mr Robert Lowell.

25 June 1964
['Rilke, Blisters and All'. J. R. von Salis, *Rainer Maria Rilke: The Years in Switzerland*. Tr. by N. K. Cruickshank. Hogarth Press]

[This is] a dogged, pedestrian book which goes on and on, with tiresome repetitions, flashbacks and anticipations of events. [...] One wishes the author had learnt from Holthusen [Hans Egon Holthusen, whose Rilke monograph, often critical of Rilke as a person, was published in English by Bowes and Bowes of Cambridge in 1952] *how* to write a book about Rilke. [...]

It is an irritating book. But one irritating feature of it is not the author's fault: he of course quoted Rilke's poems in German, but the English version gives J. B. Leishman's translations. Therefore, for example, 'The Willow of Salenegg' (which Dr von Salis calls 'this vivid, objective poem which seems to be bathed in clear autumn sunlight') has such stanzas in English as

> Now the bark of that dried trunk was gaping:
> Through the arid crack one came to see
> More and more the wholly life-escaping
> Sap-forsaken void obscurity.

If the German originals had been quoted side by side with the English translations we might, for instance, actually *understand* Leishman's:

> Look, the day has slackened pace on nighing
> That last lap that leads to evening:
> Rising stood, now standing turns to lying,
> And the life down-lier's vanishing.

Dr von Salis probably cannot judge the quality of the English versions but his own translator, N. K. Cruickshank, should have advised him always to place the German poems beside the translations.

Notes on the Translations

PART I

New Poems / *Neue Gedichte I* (1907) and *Der Neuen Gedichte: anderer Teil* (1908)

ONE [written between late 1902 and early 1907]

Abishag/*Abisag*: RSP. Revised.

The Departure of the Prodigal Son/*Der Auszug des verlorenen Sohnes*: *Personal Landscape* (1944). In RSP noted as 'dropped'. No revised version seems to have survived.

The Cathedral/*Die Kathedrale*: RSP. Revised.

The Portal /*Das Portal*: Incomplete. Revised. No RS version of the third section of Rilke's poem seems to have survived, if indeed it was ever attempted.

The Rose Window/*Die Fensterrose*: RSP typescript marked 'Final version'; this version remained unpublished. A wholesale revision of 'The Catherine Wheel' as published in *SelP* (p. 21), apparently the only time an RS version of *Die Fensterrose* appeared in print.

The Capital/*Das Kapitäl*: *SelP*. Apparently no 'Final Version' attempted.

God in the Middle Ages/*Gott im Mittelalter*: *New Statesman and Nation* (1949).

The Prisoner/*Der Gefangene*: *SelP*. Unrevised.

The Panther/*Der Panther*: RSP. Revised.

A Woman's Fate/*Ein Frauen-Schicksal*: RSP typescript headed 'Final Version'; but no other version seems to have survived.

The Convalescent/*Der Genesende*: RSP typescript headed 'Final Version', but no other version seems to have survived.

The Grown-Up/*Die Erwachsene*: *SelP* (with the title 'The Adult'). RSP. Revised. Line 12 has a holograph underlining and a marginal cross beside 'awareness' (compare the next poem 'Parting'). *SelP* reads: 'over her unfolded face' here.

Parting/*Abschied*: *SelP*. RSP. Revised. With, as in the previous poem, the word 'awareness' underlined and with a cross in the margin: *SelP* has 'that once more shows/a perfect unity' straddling lines 3 and 4. RS notes that she read this revised version at a gathering of the Poetry Society in Leicester in October 1973.

Experience of Death/*Todes-Erfahrung*: *SelP*. RSP. Revised.

Blue Hydrangea/*Blaue Hortensie*: *Springtime* (1953). Barnstone (revised). RSP (revised again). It seems RS may either have attempted or considered a version of the companion poem in *New Poems II* 'Pink Hydrangea', but no copy of it survives in her papers.

The Steps of the Orangerie/*Die Treppe der Orangerie*: *The Listener* (1948). RSP. Revised.

The Merry-Go-Round/ *Das Karrussell*: *The Listener* (1951). RSP. Revised.

Spanish Dancer/*Spanische Tänzerin*: *SelP*. *Springtime* (1953, revised). RSP. Revised again.

The Square/ *Der Platz*: *SelP*. RSP. Revised.

The Island/*Die Insel*: *Personal Landscape* (1944). RSP typescript incorporating one (two?) hand written correction(s).

Orpheus. Eurydice. Hermes/*Orpheus. Eurydike. Hermes*: *SelP*. RSP. Revised.

Alcestis/*Alkestis*: *SelP*. RSP. Revised typescript incorporates holograph corrections.

The Birth of Venus/*Geburt der Venus*: *SelP* is a revision of the text that had appeared only a few months earlier in the June 1942 issue (Number Three) of *Personal Landscape* which lacked the line 'And thus the goddess landed'. The version chosen for Robin Fedden's edition of *Personal Landscape: an anthology of exile* (1947) is that of *SelP*, not of the text that appeared in the magazine. The RSP typescript matches *SelP*, except where it has one illegible holograph correction in pencil.

Archaic Torso of Apollo /*Archaïscher Torso Apollos*: *The Citadel* (Cairo, 1942). *The Listener* (1947). RSP typescript with holograph corrections.

The Death of the Beloved / *Der Tod der Geliebten*: *SelP*. Unrevised, but in later listings RS references 'The Death of the Loved One', a title, and perhaps a version, which seems not to have survived, and which may well have been deliberately jettisoned.

A Sibyl / *Eine Sibylle*: *SelP*. RSP typescript. Revised.

The Insane in the Garden / *Irre im Garten*: *SelP* (as 'Insane in the Garden'). *Atlantic Anthology* (unrevised). Flores (revised). RSP typescript. Revised again. RS read this 'Final Version' at a gathering of the Poetry Society in Leicester in October 1973.

Unknown Family / *Fremde Familie*: *SelP*. RSP typescript. Revised.

Washing the Corpse / *Leichen-Wäsche*: *SelP* (as 'Washing a Corpse'). *The Listener* (1954, revised) as 'Washing a Dead Man'. RSP typescript. Revised again.

The Blind Man / *Der Blinde*: *Personal Landscape* (1942). *SelP*. *The Listener* (1948, revised). RSP typescript. Revised again. RS read this 'Final Version' at a gathering of the Poetry Society in Leicester in October 1973.

Late Autumn in Venice / *Spätherbst in Venedig*: *Personal Landscape* (1942). *SelP*. *New Road* (1944). *Atlantic Anthology* (unrevised). *Springtime* (1953, revised). Barnstone (revised again). RSP typescript (as Barnstone). RS read this 'Final Version' at a gathering of the Poetry Society in Leicester in October 1973.

The Ball / *Der Ball*: *SelP*. RSP. Revised.

The Child / *Das Kind*: *SelP*. *The Listener* (1950). RSP typescript. Revised.

The Dog / *Der Hund*: RSP. Final version, revised from version in *The Listener* (1948).

[RS's dates for the composition and/or revision of the original poems]

The First Elegy (1912) ['Who, if I cried out …'/'*Wer, wenn ich schriee* …']: This 1953 version (published in *Springtime*) seems to have been left unrevised by Ruth, after the numerous holograph additions that she had made to the *Poetry London* (1947) text of the poem, some of which, but by no means all, were either adopted or adapted over the six or so years intervening. The 1947 text itself shows significant revision of the version in *SelP*.

The Second Elegy (1912) ['Every angel is terrible'/'*Jeder Engel ist schrecklich*']: RS made several handwritten corrections to the *Poetry London* (1947) version, which are incorporated here; but she seems not to have returned to this elegy in later years. The 1947 version significantly revises the text that appeared in *SelP*.

The Third Elegy (1912–1913) ['One thing to sing the loved one …'/'*Eines ist, die Geliebte zu singen* …']: The latest complete version is in *Springtime* (1953) and, by virtue of being complete, has to be and has been chosen for at least part of our copy text. An incomplete revision of this Third Elegy was typed on the reverse side (and reversing the top and bottom of the page) of the Leishman text entitled 'Rolling pearls'—in Ruth's version 'Pearls will roll' [see Poems 1912–1926]—in his translation, which the Hogarth Press had published in *Selected Works II: Poetry* in 1960. RS's variant version offers an exceptionally interesting glimpse of how she went about her work, and is very much in the spirit of Rilke's opening admonition in *Sonette an Orpheus* II, 12: 'Strive for transformation'. But a much later, also incomplete, revision (headed 'New Version') offers what is, as far as it goes, in many ways preferable to all her earlier versions (there are more of this Elegy than of any of the others). We have therefore printed, for the first time, what survives of her 'New Version' as found in RSP, and where this text ends we have added the remainder of the poem from *Springtime*. The *Poetry London* printing (1947) revises *SelP*, and is itself revised for *Springtime* (1953).

The Fourth Elegy (1915) ['O tree of life, when are you wintry?'/'*O Baume lebens, o wann winterlich?*']: A composite text, respecting for the most part the *Poetry London* (1947) version, but adopting RS's numerous handwritten corrections to it, the whole text differing from the version in *SelP*, which was left unrevised for the *Atlantic Anthology* two years later. This version also incorporates where applicable what survives of an incomplete typewritten version (upside down on the reverse of a typed version of Leishman's 1960 version of 'Rolling pearls': see note to *The Third Elegy*, above), principally because it must reflect RS's later thoughts, even though the single leaf, which in fact in large part faithfully follows the *Poetry London* version, with only one holograph alteration, is crossed through. *SelP* contains the first four Elegies only, suggesting that by December 1942 RS had not yet attempted the final six; but versions of all ten existed, and had been published severally or individually, by 1947.

The Fifth Elegy (1922) ['But who, tell me, *are* they ...'/ '*Wie aber sind sie, sag mir* ...']: From the text in *Poetry London* (1947), incorporating RS's holograph corrections. This is an Elegy which RS does not seem to have further revised.

The Sixth Elegy (1912, 1914 and 1922) ['Fig-tree, for me it has so long been ...'/'*Feigenbaum, seit wie lange schon* ...']: Published, as here, from *Poetry London* (1947). RS does not appear to have worked on it again.

The Seventh Elegy (1922) ['Wooing no longer, not wooing ...'/ '*Werbung nicht mehr, nicht Werbung* ...']: Reprinted here from *Poetry London* (1947) with one small holograph alteration from RSP.

The Eighth Elegy [to Rudolf Kassner] (1922) ['The eyes of all the living creatures see the open.'/'*Mit allen Eigen sieht* ...']: The RSP typescript (headed 'Final Version) was the copy text for J. M. Cohen's 1983 *Rider Book of Mystical Verse*, which also included her 'Final Version' of the Tenth Elegy (see below). RS has added one holograph change to it ('see' for 'to look at', which has been preferred here, in line 8). RS's previous version was published in the magazine *Nine* (1950). This was the only one of her versions of the Elegies not to be published in *Poetry London* in 1947, but as an imprint they had published a version of it in the *Personal Landscape* Anthology of 1945, a magazine in which it had not in fact appeared.

The Ninth Elegy (1913, 1922) ['Why, when this set time of life …'/'*Warum, wenn es angeht …*']: Published as here in *Poetry London* (1947). RS apparently never worked on it again.

The Tenth Elegy (1912, 1914, 1922) ['May I, when at the end …'/'*Dass ich dereinst, an dem Ausgang …*']: The RSP typescript (headed 'Final Version') was used as the copy text for J. M. Cohen's 1983 anthology *The Rider Book of Mystical Verse*. RS left it unrevised, noting that the word *pshent* meant 'the Pharaonic crown symbolizing the unity of Upper and Lower Egypt'. She pointed out at the end that it had been previously published (with alterations at various stages) in: *Poetry London* (1947), in Flores and in the PEN magazine *Arena* in 1963.

from Sonnets to Orpheus/*Sonette an Orpheus* (1922)

ONE

RS notes the complete suite (26 sonnets) as having been written between the 2nd and the 5th of February 1922. The last of these sonnets was in fact added to the suite later, on the 13th of February, after the despatch to the publisher of the first 25.

I ['A tree ascended there. …'/'*Da stieg ein Baum….*']: Only version. RSP. Unpublished.

II ['A maiden almost …'/'*Und fast ein Madchen…*']: *SelP*. Revised as per the Tiller emendations (MS 2492, Box 2)

III ['A god can do it. …'/'*Ein Gott vermags. …*']: RSP. Unpublished.

IV ['You who love tenderly …'/'*O ihr Zärtlichen…*']: *SelP*. RSP. Revised.

V ['Set up no stone…'/'*Errichtet keinen Denkstein.*']: *Sel P*. RSP. Revised.

VII ['Praising…'/ '*Rühmen, das ists!*'] *SelP*. RSP Revised.

XI ['Look at the sky. …'/'*Sieh den Himmel.* …']: *SelP. New Road* (1944; no textual changes). RSP. Revised.

[XII In *Art and the Creative Unconscious* (1960) Erich Neumann quotes from Ruth's 'unpublished' version of this sonnet (p.199; '*Heil dem Geist…*' in the original German) the phrase 'For we live truly in figures'. No version of sonnet XII as a whole seems to be extant.]

XIV ['We share our days…'/'*Wir gehen um…*']: *The Citadel. SelP.* RSP. Revised.

XVI ['You, my friend…'/'*Du, mein Freund…*']: RSP. Unpublished.

XVIII ['Lord, do you hear …'/'*Hörst du das Neue…*']: *SelP.* RSP. Revised.

XX ['But, Master, o what …'/'*Dir aber, Herr, o was…*']: *SelP.* RSP. Revised.

XXIII ['O only *then* …'/'*O erst* dann…']: *SelP.* RSP. Revised.

XXIV ['Shall we disown …'/'*Sollen wir…werbenden*']: *SelP. Springtime.* Flores. RSP. Revised.

XXV ['Once more will I now …'/'*Dich aber will ich nun…*']: RSP. Unpublished.

XXVI ['You, the divine one whose song …'/'*Du aber, Gottlicher, du…*']: RSP. Unpublished.

TWO

RS notes that the complete suite (29 sonnets) was written between the 11th and 20th of February 1922. However, the 15th to 23rd of February seems now to be accepted.

II ['As at times…'/'*So wie dem Meister…*']: *SelP.* Only version. Unrevised.

IV ['This is the creature…'/'*O dieses ist das Tier…*']: *SelP. The Listener* (revised). RSP. Revised again.

V ['Flower-muscle…'/ '*Blumenmuskel…*']: *SelP.* RSP. Revised.

VI ['Rose, enthroned…'/ '*Rose, du thronende…*']: Barnstone. RSP. Revised?

VIII ['You, so few …'/ *'Wenige ihr…'*]: *Personal Landscape. SelP. Springtime* (revised). RSP. Revised.

IX ['You, who give judgment …'/ *'Rühmt euch, ihr Richtenden…'*]: *SelP.* RSP. Revised.

XII ['Strive for transformation. …' /*'Wolle die Wandlung …'*]: *SelP.* This is the (revised) version that Erich Neumann describes as 'unpublished' in his *Art and the Creative Unconscious* (1960), but there is no copy of this revision extant in RSP.

XIII ['Be ahead of all parting…'/ *'Sei allem Abschied voran…'*] RSP. Only version.

XV ['O fountain-mouth …' / *'O Brunnen-Mund…'*]: RSP. Only version.

XVII ['Where, in what ever …' / *'Wo, in welchen immer…'*]: *Personal Landscape. SelP.* Flores (revised). RSP (revised again).

XIX ['Gold dwells somewhere …' / *'Irgendwo wohnt das Gold'*]: *Personal Landscape. SelP.* RSP (revised, with a 'Former Version' attached, ending '… Only for him who sings, sayable. Audible only to gods').

XX ['Between the stars, what a distance…' / *'Zwischen den Sternen, wie weit…'*]: *Personal Landscape. SelP.* RSP. Revised.

XXI ['Sing the gardens …' / *'Singe die Gärten…'*]: RSP typescript, revised from an earlier one. But what may possibly be a later version still, a typescript with holograph corrections headed 'type', twice alters the opening two lines of the first quatrain. There are no known published versions to settle which version of XXI Ruth preferred, but the handwritten evidence may perhaps be decisive in favour of the version headed 'type'. Presumably some of these *very* difficult sonnets—in a poetic genre which invariably generates complexity—made an already demanding job even more challenging, which may also help to explain why some twenty sonnets [I: VI; VIII; IX; X; XII; XIII; XV; XVII; XIX; XXI; XXII/ II: I; III; VII; X; XI; XIV; XVI; XVIII; XXIX] were apparently never attempted.

XXII ['O in spite of Fate...' / '*O trotz Schicksal...*']: *Forum* (Jerusalem). *SelP. Atlantic Anthology* (unrevised).

XXIII ['Call me ...' / '*Rufe mich...*']: *SelP. Springtime* (revised). Flores (as *Springtime*, but with initial capitalizations in every line). RSP. Again revised.

XXIV ['O this delight, ever new ...' / '*O diese Lust, immer neu...*']: RSP typescript with holograph corrections. Ruth corrected what she called an 'Old Version. Never published' in line 1 (originally 'clay'), line 3 (originally 'Nonetheless, there rose towns'), line 11 (originally 'transcending') and line 13 (originally 'he' was left unitalicised).

XXV ['Listen ...' / '*Schon, horch, hörst du...*']: RSP. Unpublished. Only version.

XXVI ['How it grips us ...' / '*Wie ergreift uns...*']: RSP. Unpublished. Ruth was apparently dissatisfied with the phrasing of the run-on from lines 7–8. An earlier version reads: 'crevasses / In that same space'.

XXVIII ['O come and go. ...' / '*O komm und geh. ...*']: RSP. Unpublished. Only version.

XXIX ['Silent friend ...' / '*Stiller Freund...*']: *SelP.* Unrevised.

PART II

Whilst we have preserved the intertwined lines of Rilke's development, as reflected in his published volumes, we have placed his earlier poems (those which RS translated) *after* what is widely, and surely rightly, regarded as his first fully mature collection of poems (the *Neue Gedichte*; New Poems). Her Cairo *Selected Poems* of 1942 begins with four of the relatively early poems from *Das Stunden-Buch* (The Book of Hours) which may themselves be the earliest versions RS attempted (her signature in her own copy, a 1936 reprint, bears the dateline 'Kairo 1939'). But she would have been the first to agree that Rilke, although a prolific writer throughout his relatively short life, took time to develop into what he became, having put together either in manuscript or in privately published volumes, several collections earlier than *Das Stunden-Buch*, in none of which Ruth seems to have taken any active interest, and many of which may either have been unknown to her, or virtually impossible for her to acquire. No translations by RS of the first section ('The Book of the Monastic Life') of the triptych-like *Book of Hours* survive in her papers, but she numbered and marked more than sixty of the one hundred-and-fifty-plus unnumbered poems in the collection, with the lack of numbers apparently most keenly felt in that first and largest section, and in the subsequent sections increasingly trying to identify what for her were the most interesting ones, or perhaps the ones (in some cases certainly the ones) which she would go on to translate. She knew her early Rilke well, and indeed speaks warmly of *Das Stunden-Buch* (if not of its translator) in a TLS review. But the Rilke that really mattered to her, as to most others before and since, is the more fully formed poet, by no means free of 'foibles and absurdities', but with his poetic utterance refined and focused in spite of them.

from The Book of Images/*Das Buch der Bilder*
(published July 1902, augmented edition December 1906)

THE FIRST BOOK: PART ONE
'Whoever you may be…' / *Eingang*: *The Listener* (1950). RSP. Revised.

Childhood / *Kindheit*: *Personal Landscape*. SelP. RSP. Revised typescript with holograph corrections almost all of which correspond to the changes listed by Terence Tiller as having been written by him into his copy of the Cairo book (UoR MS 2492, Box 2).

THE FIRST BOOK: PART TWO

People at Night /*Menschen bei Nacht*: SelP (*as* People by Night). RSP. Revised.

Anxiety / *Bangnis*: RSP. Revised.

'Loneliness is like a rain ...' / *Einsamkeit*: The Listener (1954). RSP. Unrevised.

Autumn Day / *Herbstag*: SelP. *The Egyptian Gazette* (1943). *The Listener* (1948). RSP typescript with holograph corrections.

Evening / *Abend*: SelP. RSP. Revised typescript with holograph corrections.

THE SECOND BOOK: PART TWO

Fragments from Lost Days / *Fragmente auf den verlorenen Tagen*: SelP. RSP. Revised, with holograph corrections.

from The Book of Hours/*Das Stunden-Buch*
(published December 1905)

THE BOOK OF PILGRIMAGE [sequence of poems written between 15 September and 25 September 1901]

[V–VI] 'To you, my praying ...' / '*Dir ist mein Beten keine Blasphemie*' and '*Und seine Sorgfalt ist uns wie ein Alb* ...': RSP typescript incorporating holograph corrections. Unpublished.

[IX–X] 'You are the heir...' / '*Du bist der Erbe* ...' and '*Un du erbst das grün* ...': SelP. RSP. Revised.

[XI] 'I'm merely one...' / '*Ich bin nur einer* ...': SelP. RSP typescript with holograph corrections. Unpublished.

[XXXII] 'Now the red rowans...' / '*Jetzt reifen schon die roten Berberitzen* ...': SelP. The Listener (1949). RSP. Revised typescript with holograph changes.

[XXXIII] 'God have no fear ...' / '*Du musst nicht bangen, Gott* ...': SelP as 'Be not afraid, God ...'. RSP. Revised.

[XXXIV] 'I dig for you...' / '*In tiefen Nächten* ...': RSP. Unpublished.

THE BOOK OF POVERTY AND DEATH [sequence of poems written between 13 April and 20 April 1903]

[IV–V] '... Lord, the large cities ...' / '*Denn, Herr, die grossen Städte sind*...': RSP. Revised typescript with holograph corrections. Unpublished. RS notes that she read a version of this poem at George Fraser's in September 1952.

[VIII] 'Lord, we are poorer...' / *'Herr, wir sind ärmer ...'*: *SelP*. RSP. Revised.

from *Uncollected and Later Poems* (1912–1926)

Apparition [Spring 1912] / *Erscheinung*: *The Listener* (1950). Barnstone (revised). RSP. Revised again.

'Pearls roll down ...' [July–December 1912] / *'Perlen entrollen ...'*: *SelP*. RSP revised, holograph corrections to typescript.

The Spanish Trilogy [I and II only] [January 1913] / *Die Spanische Trilogie*: [Poems I and II only. No version of poem III seems to be extant.] RSP typescript.

A Spring (Paris) [April 1913] / *Frühling*: *The Listener* (1949). RSP. Revised.

Christ's Descent into Hell [April 1913] / *Christi Höllenfahrt*: *SelP*. Unrevised, but later RS listings re-title this poem 'The Harrowing of Hell', which may suggest attempts at revision, none of which is now extant. Other indications, however, suggest that she was content to jettison her attempt(s) at a version.

'Behind the guiltless trees ...' [August 1913] / *'Hinter den schuld-losen Bäumen ...'*: RSP. No other extant version. Unpublished.

The Great Night [January 1914] / *Die grosse Nacht*: RSP typescript, with no revisions. Unpublished.

'"One must die ..."' [9 July 1914] / *'"Man muss sterben ..."'*: *SelP*. Never reprinted.

'Beloved ...' [winter 1913–1914] / *'Du im Voraus ...'*: *The Citadel*. *SelP*. *The Listener* (1949; revised). RSP typescript. Revised again.

'Exposed on the hills ...' [September 1914]/ *'Ausgezetzt auf den Bergen ...'*: RSP typescript. No corrections. Unpublished.

'Again and again ...' [1914] / *'Immer wieder ...'*: RSP
typescript. No corrections. Unpublished.

'Music: breathing of statues ...' [January 1918] / *'Musik:
Atem der Statuen ...'*: RSP typescript incorporating a
holograph correction in line 9 typed as 'presses outward',
and—handwritten—'do it'. This is followed by a much freer
version in RS's hand headed 'Flores' (possibly intended for his
Anchor anthology, in which neither of these versions appear),
presumably superseded by this typescript:

Music: breathing of statues. Perhaps
stillness of pictures. Language where languages
end. Time,
erect on the pathology of hearts
towards extraction.

Feelings for whom? Transformation
of feelings into what? Into audible landscape.
Strange land: Music. Space grown from our hearts,
ours most intimate,
stepping beyond us,
striving afar.

       Sacred farewell,
when the within is around us as distance most distant,
Air's other side,
pure,
gigantic,
and not for us to inhabit.

Neither of her versions appeared in print. Both of them differ
strikingly from, and perhaps improve on, Leishman, a typed-
out version of whose text is attached to one of them.

'When catching what you throw ...' [January 1922] / *'Solang
du Selbstgeworfenes fängst ...'*: SelP as 'As long as you catch what
you throw yourself ...'. RSP. Revised typescript.

Imaginary Life [September 1923] / *Imaginärer Lebenslauf*: SelP.
RSP. Revised typescript.

The Magician [February 1924] / *Der Magier*: SelP. Described
in RSP as 'dropped', which, with no evidence of revision or
of submission to editors, may suggest that the translator had

at some point decided to jettison this, or not to attempt to re-publish it in any version. In other listings made by Ruth this poem is only one of many versions either blocked out or crossed out, but most of those (unlike this one) are poems to which she returned and which she revised assiduously. What may well be her one attempt at revision of this version is, as adopted here, of the last sentence (replacing 'Bound is also he'), as handwritten by Terence Tiller into his copy of the Cairo *SelP*.

A NOTE ON TRANSLATIONS NOT FOUND

There follows a list of titles of Rilke versions by RS either left unfinished, or jettisoned, or lost, or unobtainable:

from *Das Buch der Bilder:*
[purchased by RS in Haifa early in 1942]:

II: I

In the Certosa / *In der Certosa* (ticked in the margin in RS's copy, as all the surviving versions from this volume are)

II: II

A Night of Storm / *Aus einem Sturmnacht* (marginal tick, as above)

The Blind Girl / *Die Blinde* (marginal tick, as above)

from *Neue Gedichte* (1907):

Roman Fountain / *Römische Fontäne*

from *Der Neuen Gedichte anderer Teil* (1908):

A Portrait / *Bildnis* is listed by RS as published in *Forum*, Jerusalem, 1944, along with three other poems which do appear there, but not found there and later described as 'dropped', presumably by the editors.

Pink Hydrangea / *Rosa Hortensie*

from Uncollected Poems 1912 to 1926:

The Fruit / *Die Frucht*

and (possibly) from *Das Stunden-Buch*:

III: 14 / *'Denn Gärten sind,—von Köningen gebaut...'*

A CUMULATIVE CHECKLIST

The following list gives details of when and where the Ruth Speirs translations of Rilke first appeared in print (omitting reprints whether revised or unrevised):

1942
The Citadel (Cairo):

Sonnets to Orpheus I/XIV

'Beloved ...'

Archaic Torso of Apollo

Personal Landscape [Cairo] Number Three (June 1942):

The Birth of Venus

The Panther

The Blind Man

Late Autumn in Venice

Parting

Spanish Dancer

Personal Landscape [Cairo], Volume One, Part Four (October 1942)

Abishag

Childhood

Sonnets to Orpheus II/VIII, XVII, XIX, XX

Selected Poems (in addition to the titles listed above) [December; The Anglo-Egyptian Bookshop, Cairo]:

'You are the heir ...'

'Now the red rowans ...'

'Lord: we are poorer ...'

People at Night [*as* People by Night]

Anxiety

Autumn Day

Evening

Fragments from Lost Days

The Cathedral

The Rose Window [*as* The Catherine Wheel]

The Prisoner

The Grown-Up [*as* The Adult]

Experience of Death

The Square

Orpheus. Eurydice. Hermes

Alcestis

The Death of the Beloved

A Sibyl

The Insane in the Garden [*as* Insane in the Garden]

Unknown Family

The Ball

The Child

The Duino Elegies: First, Second, Third, Fourth

Sonnets to Orpheus I/II, IV, V, VII, XI, XVIII, XX, XXIII

Sonnets to Orpheus II/II, IV, V, IX, XII, XXII, XXIII, XXIX

Christ's Descent into Hell

'Pearls will roll …' [*as* 'Pearls roll down …']

'"One must die …"'

'Whenever you catch …' [*as* 'As long as you catch …']

Imaginary Life

The Magician

[By December 1942 there were versions of more than half of the Rilke poems RS was ever to publish, but any item which had not been 'dropped' or abandoned underwent significant revision over the next twenty and more years.]

1944
Personal Landscape [Cairo] Volume Two, Part Two:

The Departure of the Prodigal Son

The Island (North Sea)

Forum [Palestine Broadcasting Company, Jerusalem]:

'Whoever you may be …'

The Steps of the Orangerie [*as* The Staircase of the Orangerie]

1945
Personal Landscape [an anthology published in London by Editions Poetry London]:

The Duino Elegies: The Eighth, which had *not* appeared in the Cairo magazine, and which was also conspicuous by its absence from the two consecutive issues of *Poetry London* in which the other *Elegies* were subsequently to appear in sequence: Sept/Oct 1947 [revised versions of The First, Second, Third, Fourth] and Nov/Dec 1947 [see next entry].

1947
Poetry London Volume Three, Number Twelve
(November/December):

The Duino Elegies: The Fifth, Sixth, Seventh, Ninth, Tenth

1948
The Listener:

The Dog [5 August]

1949
The Listener:

A Spring (Paris) [2 June]

The New Statesman and Nation

God in the Middle Ages [3 December]

1950
The Listener:

The Child [5 January]

Apparition [5 January]

1951
The Listener:

The Merry-Go-Round [26 July]

1953
Springtime, edited by G S Fraser and Iain Fletchter
(Peter Owen, April 1953):

Blue Hydrangea

1954
The Listener:

'Loneliness is like …' [16 December]

1966

Willis Barnstone (ed.) *Modern European Poetry*(Bantam Books, New York):

Sonnets to Orpheus II/VI

All other titles are published here for the first time. After each poem we indicate whether revision occurred, but it has not been considered necessary to particularise the precise alterations except in a few special instances.

BROADCASTS

Palestine Broadcasting Company (27 October 1943):

The Panther

The Duino Elegies [either the Third or the Fourth]

BBC Third Programme (29 March 1951, repeated 31 March 1951 and 21 August 1951):

Autumn Day

Childhood

Fragments from Lost Days

Sonnets to Orpheus I/II

BBC Third Programme (29 July 1968):

Spanish Dancer

Two Rivers Press has been publishing in and about Reading since 1994. Founded by the artist Peter Hay (1951–2003), the press continues to delight readers, local and further afield, with its varied list of individually designed, thought-provoking books.